Ratiocination

Weaving the Threads of Grammar, Revision, and Editing

Ratiocination

Weaving the Threads of Grammar, Revision, and Editing

Joyce Armstrong Carroll, Ed.D., H.L.D

with

Becky Coker, Emily E. Smith, & other voices

Foreword by Joan Wink

Spring, TX

Copyright © 2011 Joyce Armstrong Carroll

All rights reserved. No part of this publication may be reproduced, transmitted, or stored in an information retrieval system in any form or by any means, graphic, electronic, or mechanical, including photocopying, taping, and recording without prior written permission from the publisher.

ISBN 10- 1-888842-09-1
ISBN 13 - 978-1-888842-09-8

Printed in the United States of America

Requests for permission to make copies
of any part of the work should be mailed to:

Permissions
Absey & Co. Inc.
23011 Northcrest
Spring, Texas 77389

Visit us at www.Absey.biz
If you would like the authors to conduct inservice based upon **Ratiocination: Weaving the Threads of Grammar and Revision** contact them through: www.absey.biz Or contact the author at: drjac@abydoslearning.org

ra·ti·oc·i·nate (rsh-s-nt)
intr.v. ra·ti·oc·i·nat·ed, ra·ti·oc·i·nat·ing, ra·ti·oc·i·nates
To reason methodically and logically.
[Latin raticinr, raticint-, from rati, calculation; see ratio.]
rati·oci·nation n.
rati·oci·nator n.

The American Heritage® Dictionary of the English Language, Fourth Edition copyright ©2000 by Houghton Mifflin Company. Updated in 2009. Published by Houghton Mifflin Company. All rights reserved.

ratiocinate [ˌrætɪˈɒsɪˌneɪt]
vb
(intr) to think or argue logically and methodically; reason
[from Latin ratiōcinārî to calculate, from ratiō reason]
ratiocination n
ratiocinative adj
ratiocinator n

Collins English Dictionary – Complete and Unabridged © HarperCollins Publishers 1991, 1994, 1998, 2000, 2003

He'd run in debt by disputation,
And pay with **ratiocination.**
    Hudibras. Part I, Canto I, Line 77, Samuel Butler

When it is impossible to stretch the very elastic threads of historical **ratiocination** any farther, when actions are clearly contrary to all that humanity calls right or even just, the historians produce a saving conception of "greatness."
    --*War and Peace,* Leo Tolstoy

We know that for logicians (formerly at any rate) the concept is the simple and primitive element; next comes the judgment, uniting two or several concepts; then **ratiocination**, combining two or several judgments.
    --*The Analysis of Mind,* Bertrand Russell

CONTENTS

FOREWORD
iv

PREFACE
xv
How Ratiocination Began

THE PREQUEL
xix
Ratiocination and Revision or Clues in the Written Draft (From *English Journal*, November 1982 by the National Council of Teachers of English. Reprinted with permission.)

SECTION ONE
Foundations
1

Chapter One: The Roots of Ratiocination   2

- Setting the Scene   2
- Grammar Within the Writing Process   2
- Ratiocination's Roots   3
   - *American Literature* 3 ❦ *The "Balloons" of S. W. Clark* 3 ❦ *The Diagramming of Reed and Kellogg* 5 ❦ *The Learning Theories of Vygotsky, Bruner, and Emig* 7 ❦ *The Philosophy of John Dewey* 15 ❦ *Sentence Combining and Generative Rhetoric* 16 ❦ *Brain Research Meets Ratiocination* 17 ❦ *Rhetoric* 23
- I Rest My Case   24

Chapter Two: Teaching Ratiocination   25

- Setting the Scene   25
   - ❦ *Determining What to Ratiocinate: Ten Guidelines* 25
- The Ten Guidelines in Action   27
   - ❦ *Beginning Writers – Coordinating Conjunctions* 27
- I Rest My Case   40

- ❦ *Intermediate Writers—Relative Pronouns* 40
- I Rest My Case   53
   - ❦ *Advanced Writers--Verbals* 54
- I Rest My Case   58

SECTION TWO
Mentoring Lessons
59

- Setting the Scene   60

Chapter Three: Emergent Revision—Shawn and Jon   61
   ❦ *Mentoring Lesson One: Beginning Sentences with Upper Case Letters and Ending with Terminal Punctuation* 61 ❦ *Mentoring Lesson Two: The OU Vowel Sound* 66

Chapter Four: Transitional Revision—Moving from Imitative to Cognitive Understanding of Grammar and Syntactical Structures—Amanda and Marianna   73
   ❦ *Mentoring Lesson Three: Quotation Marks and Commas with the Tag in Dialogue* 78 ❦ *Mentoring Lesson Four: "To Be" Vebs* 84

Chapter Five: Medial Revision—On-level Understanding of Grammatical and Syntactical Structures—Stephen and Nellie   91
- The Original Writing (before)   92
- Grammar/revision/editing Opportunities   93
   ❦ *Prioritizing* 94 ❦ *The Rationcination Strategy for Sentences* 94
   ❦ *The Rationcination Strategy for Transitions* 95 ❦ *Possible Lessons* 96
- Revised Writing (after)   102
   ❦ *Evaluation* 102 ❦ *What Did We Learn from Stephen's Rationcination?* 103
- The Original Writing (before)   104
   ❦ *An Analysis* 105
- Grammar/revision/editing Opportunities   105
   ❦ *Prioritizing* 106 ❦ *Rationcinating Verbs* 106
- The Highlighted Version   108
   ❦ *Possible Lessons*
- Revised Writing (after)   111
   ❦ *Evaluation*

Chapter Six: Elevated Revision—Genuine Conceptual Understanding, Reaching Grammatical and Syntactical Maturity in Style, Tone, Craft--Alexandra   113

- The Original Writing of the First Paragraph   114
  - ❦ *An Analysis* 115
- Grammar/revision/editing Opportunities   115
  - ❦ *Prioritizing* 116 ❦ *Rationcinating for the Thesis Statement* 116
  - ❦ *Possible Lessons* 118
- Revised Writing (after)   119
  - ❦ *Evaluation* 121
- I Rest My Case   122

Ratiocination References   123

SECTION THREE
Thoughtful Practitioners
125

Chapter Seven: Reverse + Ratiocination = Revertiocination   Emily E. Smith
127

Chapter Eight: Ratiocination in the High School Classroom   Becky Coker
151

SECTION FOUR
Other Voices
167

Chapter Nine: Ratiocination and Teaching Tone   Shirley Blanton
169

Chapter Ten: Successful Revision Demands Writer's Discretion   Sonja Edwards
185

Chapter Eleven: Figurative Language Meets Ratiocination   Jean Ewer Hawsey
197

Chapter Twelve: Ratiocination: Supporting the Writing Life   Judy Wallis
212

CODA
The Legacy of Ratiocination
217

FOREWORD

Often times it seems that the book we need finds us at the exact moment when our need is the greatest. Maybe it feels like we choose a book, but in reality, the book chooses us. This is exactly what happened to me, when Joyce Armstrong Carroll invited me to read her new book about ratiocination and write a foreword for it.

"Sure," I responded, "but first, what does ratiocination mean?" It was a mystery to me, even though I was smack dab in the middle of living it, without realizing. You see, I was rewriting and revising a manuscript, which had gone dormant for a few years. I felt like I was drowning in the ambiguity of my own old manuscript. I was looking for clues to rebuild it in a more logical, more precise format. After reading Carroll's new book, I now have the clues of ratiocination to help me solve my own mystery.

What do real writers do? We write, and we revise. Ratiocination is a process, which will help me improve my own revision today. Bingo! It is exactly what I need at the very moment when I need it—the book found me. And, it will help you and the students in your classes think more logically, more clearly, as Joyce Armstrong Carroll and her colleagues show us how to integrate grammar with revisions.

Words matter. Oh, those beautiful words. How we love them. It is this love of language, which makes the mystery of writing and rewriting so alluring, so inviting, and so contagious. If we are driven by the magic of language, our students will see it, feel it, and emulate it. In addition, through these pages, Carroll reminds us to always embed the integration of grammar and revision in the language of the students.

Solving your own mystery: That is what is going to happen to you as you read this book.

It's true: I read Edgar Allen Poe, too, but I didn't learn this great new word, ratiocination. Carroll did because she found ratiocination in the context of a great mystery as the fictional character, Dupin, needed to ratiocinate to solve

Foreword

the puzzling events in the Poe stories. If you fell in love with Nancy Drew books, you, too, learned to look for clues and see the connections as you sleuthed with Nancy. If you are a fan of mystery books today, you are ratiocinating every time while predicting what will happen on the next page. As teachers, we love to see students follow clues, use logic, put all of the pieces of a puzzle together, in order to experience an "A-ha" moment of clarity and understanding. As writers, we continually ratiocinate when we rewrite, rethink, and revise. We do this to paint a more vivid, meaningful image for our readers.

Ratiocinating and writing: this is exactly where Carroll and her co-authors take us in this fascinating book about grammar. First, a confession: I love grammar, which only proves that there is no accounting for taste. I have known some who find grammar to be incomprehensible, irrelevant, or tedious. We, in schools, have been known to teach it twelve straight years in a row, and some students still do not understand it.

Carroll shows us new keys to unravel the mystery of writing and revision, as she provides "comprehensible input" on grammar. She not only gives us clues to help us in revision, she also provides visual structures so that we "see" our own process. Throughout the book, Joyce Armstrong Carroll keeps a bright spotlight on the writing of the students, because their own words matter most to them at that particular moment in learning.

Writing is thinking. As we write, we get smarter because we focus on making our thoughts meaningful for others, the readers. If it doesn't matter to the readers, it doesn't matter, even if the writer knows exactly what she means. As if weaving her own narrative tapestry, Carroll traces the historical roots of ratiocination back to a few of our favorites: Vygotsky, Dewey, Emig, Smith, Lakoff, and many others. Her connections (dare I say, her *winklinks*) are vivid and visual. As I read, I found myself thinking: "Hey, I never thought of that before."

Vygtosky's notions of play, concept formation, scaffolding, modeling, and collaboration come to life with Carroll's *winklinks* to ratiocination. She shows us that as students "play" with the visual integration of grammar and writing, they are also growing cognitively. Ratiocination helps learners become "a head taller" than they were yesterday. We, adults, are the same: As we "play" with our words, we think more deeply. As I read Carroll's manuscript, I "played" with the ideas and grew "a head taller."

Joan Wink

    Teachers will immediately see the value of the *Ten Guidelings* to the curriculum of the classroom. No matter what we teach, we are all writing teachers, and I will share this Top Ten list this week with my beginning teacher credential students. In addition, I have found many other specific, step-by-step guidelines to turning the theory of this book into the practice of the classroom. The text is filled with multiple ways of direct teaching these strategies to writers of all ages.

    Of course, we love it when we find someone who loves the same as we do. Joyce Armstrong Carroll and colleagues use the lens of ratiocination as they revise my understandings of many of the people and ideas, I love––even going so far as to help me relive my love of "bird-by-bird." But, you'll have to find that one on your own! In addition, when I finished writing the draft of this foreword, I used the "search all" feature of my little computer to find my own "to be" verbs––a humbling experience, which the readers of this text will appreciate.

                                      Joan Wink, Ph. D.
                                      Professor Emerita
                                      California State University, Stanislaus
                                      January 25, 2011

Preface

How Ratiocination Began

Fresh from graduate school, fresh from studying under Janet Emig, fresh from the concept of authentic writing, fresh from a dissertation that proved students taught by teachers schooled in writing as a process wrote better, I was filled with missionary zeal. Eager, when I presented, I would say, "And we must teach grammar within the writing process." Teachers would nod—until one day a brave teacher raised her hand and said, "Dr. Carroll, we agree with you but how do we do that?"

Remember, this was the era of teaching one semester of grammar, one semester of composition, and then literature. This was the era when we believed if we taught grammar first and then assigned writing, the kids would put 2 + 2 together. That teacher's question exposed the truth—we—teachers and students were both in a quandary about how to work the two in tandem.

At that time I was teaching college with several sections of Freshman Writing. Excitedly I'd conference with my students telling (not showing) them to do things like "develop" or "liven the verbs." Almost simultaneous to the experience with that brave teacher came an experience with a confused student. As he walked toward his desk after our conference, he muttered, "This paper is a mystery to me." That became the Eureka! moment for me. At once I realized that my advice was too general, too abstract—that any help with grammar and revision had to be integral to the writing itself. So my research began.

I worked for years developing my method of ratiocination, building upon much research and years of teaching. Trainers in the Abydos project—Doug Lemov would call them champions—also worked with ratiocination. We all began to realize that when parts of the composition were separated and then reassembled according to the rules of grammar and the meaning intended by the writer, when they were fitted together with the help of clues and cross-references, which we

How Ratiocination Began

realized needed to be made concrete so students could hunt them down as in a paper chase, we revitalized the act of revising and grammar and that made sense to students. Once in place, ratiocination revealed levels of thought in students' writing somewhat like those Russian nesting dolls and enabled even neophyte writers to grasp the purpose of grammar and the need for revision.

Over the years teachers have told me things like, "I can teach every grammar concept in my curriculum just by having the kids code and decode 'to be' verbs." "My kids actually enjoy grammar now." "Sometimes it is hard to stop them—they get so into it." "They love sharing the before and after of their writing." "They can see the improvement for themselves."

My seminal article reprinted here—my first response to that brave teacher and confused student—catapulted me into doing more research. Placed as prequel in this book, it provides the historical context. Subsequent chapters and the contributions by teachers offer a trove of further possibilities, deeper teaching, each demonstrating just how ratiocination impacts students' writing and each proving that grammar can be taught within the writing process!

—dr jac

The Prequel

Ratiocination and Revision
or
Clues in the Written Draft

Joyce Armstrong Carroll
(From *English Journal*, November 1982. Copyright 1982 by the National Council of Teachers of English. Reprinted with permission.)

Commentary:

Carroll chronicles a childhood where words and wonder were a natural part of her growing-up. Unfortunately, today's society seems to militate against childhoods where imagination and rich reading experiences abound. Day care, Little League, T-Ball, computer camp, latch-key, T.V., poverty, pull at children's lives. Helen at the Red Balloon Bookstore in San Antonio says that 10% of the American public purchase 90% of the books. In an informal survey of the parents of 150 seniors

My fascination with clues began with a Captain Marvel decoder ring. After drinking jars of Ovaltine, I collected enough labels to send for that prize. When it arrived, the clues read by the radio announcer at program's end no longer formed incomprehensible cryptograms. Eagerly I copied them; anxiously I turned the ring's painted silvery dial to decode them. Figuring every word became an adventure--every message a solved mystery.

Progressing from radio to reading, I collected Carolyn Keene's books like those Ovaltine labels. Nancy Drew, her chum Helen Corning, and I were amateur detectives. No clue escaped us. Soon, my literary tastes refining, Sherlock Holmes and Dr. Watson replaced Nancy and Helen, then Agatha Christie's Hercule Poirot became my hero--I had been well prepared for secret packets and revolutionary coups d'état. But my fascination flowered while following C. Auguste Dupin, Edgar Allan Poe's smart (and I knew handsome) sleuth, especially when I discovered the sophisticated word for this process of logically reasoning out clues--ratiocination.

Although no Holmes, Poirot, or Dupin, in one eureka! moment I realized how I apply this ratiocinative process, how like a detective I become while revising. Relentlessly I go back through my

Ratiocination and Revision or Clues in the Written Draft

writing searching for clues in the language, decoding them in order to make the writing better. For example, in an early draft, my opening sentence read: My fascination with clues may have started with a... When I reentered the writing, *may* and *have* provided clues for decoding. *May* expresses contingency; *have* indicates the perfect tense. Since I wanted certainty in the past, both proved inaccurate--the sentence had to be revised.

Students, however, do not share this relentlessness; they cower during revision as if terrorized, failing to realize that a piece of writing, like a story, is essentially over at the beginning, the crime already committed when the author introduces the clues. Usually the structure of the story revolves around the detective figuring out those clues to discover the culprit and bring the story to a satisfactory close. So, too, with a written draft in need of revision. It's an unsolved mystery. Most everything is essentially there, but the writer must reenter the writing as a detective, checking the significance of linguistic clues to bring the piece to a satisfactory close.

Students, most neophyte writers, most unskilled detectives of language, are unable to reenter their writing without clues, are unable to do revision as Frank Smith describes it in Writing and the Writer: "...review the draft of the text from their own point of view to discover what the text contains" (p. 127). Therefore students avoid revision: they abhor it and, if pressed, usually do a shoddy job of it. Directions, fine as they may be for the practiced writer, (lower the noun/verb ratio" or transform passive constructions into active ones in Linda Flower's *Problem-Solving Strategies for Writing* [New York: Harcourt, 1981, pp. 177-179]), strike students as vague or meaningless since they give no clues pointing where to begin.

Commentary:

at Cooper High School in Abilene, Texas, 47 of the seniors reported not having a single book in their homes. Thirty-two of the homes had one book—a dictionary. It is highly unlikely that these students had childhoods that were rich with literary experiences.

Knowing how to revise requires years and years of experiencing writing. Emergent writers do not readily revise. Neophyte writers struggle with revision. And the experienced writer can still find it difficult.

The Prequel: A Reprint from the English Journal

Commentary:

The teacher who approaches teaching revision by pronouncement, has the same effect on a student's writing as a politician at a national convention. Proclaiming a candidate as a "man or woman of the people" doesn't make it so. Telling isn't teaching. The uninformed, untrained teacher announced, "today you will revise your paper." Then the teacher wonders why the students did not revise. Revision must be taught in order for it to be incorporated into writing.

One good way to teach this technique makes use of a chart that shows the relationship of the code to the clue and the decoding tips. On the chalkboard the teacher can write:

If clues hold the secret to revision, then teachers must show student how to code the clues which will enable them to reenter their papers the way practiced writers do. Further, by following those coded clues and by using the process of logical reasoning to decode them, students figure out words and meanings to solve the mystery of their written drafts and bring their papers to a satisfactory close.

The Procedure

Instruct students to bring colored markers, pens, pencils, or crayons--colored coders--or keep a box of these in class. After students have shaped their prewritings (clearly labeled at the top) into trial rough drafts (also clearly labeled), introduce "Clue Day."

Present the clues (see "coding the Clues" below) that you want students to code for this paper. For example, if you want students to work on the first clue, you might list all the "to be" verbs on the board, telling students, "Each time you come across one of these verbs, circle it clearly with one color." For the next clue, they would use another color. Depending

Code	Clue	Decoding
(circle)	"to be " verbs is am are was were be being been	• do not change • change to a livelier verb • indicate passive voice • indicates a knotted, weak sentence • do not change if the "to be" verb is in a quote • consider leaving it in dialogue—characters speak this way

Ratiocination and Revision or Clues in the Written Draft

upon the length of the papers, and the number of clues, this coding process could easily take the rest of the period. What emerges are drafts clearly filled with visually coded clues.

Next, explain how decoding their clues involves logical thinking (ratiocination--although you may not wish to introduce the term at this time) as well as decision making since there are many options and alternatives available when working with language (see "The Decoding" below). After this explanation, students reenter their trial rough drafts decoding their clues, making decisions, and rewriting onto what will become their rough drafts. As students engage in decoding, the teacher may move about the room offering individual help.

When students polish their rough drafts into their final papers, they hand in all their drafts fastened together in descending order with the final paper on top. This order makes assessment easier, while the coding and the decoding make it more thorough, more specific, and quicker. Grading should be keyed directly to the concepts covered in the clues and to the quality of writing after decoding those clues.

For the first paper, I'd recommend presenting the first two clues; for the second paper, review them; then add one or two more depending upon the level and writing abilities of the students. For slow students, one clue per paper is sufficient. I have sequenced these clues in a workable order so that by the end of the semester, through this process of accumulation, all ten clues will become part of the student's repertoire. A word of caution: do not rush this giving of clues because the ratiocination which each clue generates is a highly complex and intricate transformational process.

Commentary:

A word about using the chalkboard versus using the overhead. The chalkboard invites interaction and simultaneous discovery. Presentation on the chalkboard keeps the pacing of the presentation at a comfortable rate for students.

Ratiocination guarantees that students will use:
• Higher-order thinking skills,
• Revision skills in a context, and
• Concrete signals to reenter their own writing.

With ratiocination, teachers find they use some codes, clues, and decodes every piece of discourse. In time, student writers internalize some clues. As with most good techniques, however, ratiocination can be abused.

The Prequel: A Reprint from the English Journal

Commentary:

One well-meaning teacher may insist that her students use all 10 codes, clues, and decodes on each paper they write, and the result: cognitive overload and illegible drafts. This over-teaching can be detrimental and discouraging.

One teacher told us that "to be" verbs is the only code she uses with her students. Through it she is able to teach everything from word choice and grammatical concepts to syntax and style.

Coding the Clues
1. Circle all "to be" verbs.
2. Make a wavy line under repeated words.
3. Underline each sentence.
4. Bracket each sentence beginning.
5. Draw an arrow from subject to predicate in each sentence.
6. Place a box around clichés.
7. Mark words that might be imprecise with a check.
8. X out the word very.
9. Draw two vertical lines next to anything underdeveloped.
10. Put it in a triangle.

The Decoding

1. When decoding a circle, students determine if the "to be" verb should be untouched because changing it would diminish the composition or if it should be replaced because changing it to a livelier verb would enhance the composition. Sometimes a "to be" verb signals a passive construction which might entail either revising its order to subject-verb-complement or leaving it to focus on the complement. Other times a "to be" verb suggests a weak sentence which should be omitted or drastically revised.

2. When approaching a wavy line, students consider if the repetition is necessary and should remain to make the meaning emphatic, to show continuity between sentences or paragraphs, to retain parallel form, or to make the sentence function as is the case with words such as a, an, the. If the repetition is unnecessary, it should be eliminated or changed because it reveals careless word choice or confuses by using homonymic words.

Ratiocination and Revision or Clues in the Written Draft

3. Underlining invites students to study their sentences. For example, if they are about the same length, shortening or lengthening a few adds variety and provides visual relief. If choppy (each sentence contains a minimal number of words or a simple idea divided into two or more sentences), combining sentences produces a smoother effect. If stringy (ideas are strung together with coordinating conjunctions as if all elements are equal), cutting down on conjunctions and subordinating ideas solves the problem.

4. Bracketing heightens awareness of the tendency to start each sentence with a noun or pronoun subject, thereby lowering the overall impact of the writing. Students decode by experimenting with a variety of beginnings--modifiers, phrases, clauses.

5. While most arrows will point to subject/predicate agreement, some will uncover dialect problems: I do, you do, he do, she do, it do. Using a current handbook and the student's writing, individualize instruction on this problem. Students should compare examples in handbooks with what they ten since many rules and exceptions govern these situations.

6. Students might miss boxing in all their trite expressions. Because they are so common, students use them without thinking. When they do catch a cliché, they decode the clue by asking how they could more freshly express the hackneyed.

7. Word precision problems arise when students fail to distinguish nuances of meaning. Decoding a check demands cross reference work with both thesaurus and dictionary.

Commentary:

We have learned from other teachers that this works best when the students underline the sentences in alternating colors.

See chapter 5. *Acts of Teaching,* (2nd Edition) Carroll and Wilson, Teacher's Idea Press. 2009

This is a good time to work collaboratively.

The Prequel: A Reprint from the English Journal

Commentary:

Teachers have extended this to include a lot (as one word), really, good, and other overused words.

One way to help students develop is by using charts and the SEE strategy (see chapter 6 *Acts of Teaching,* (2nd Edition) Carroll and Wilson, Teacher's Idea Press. 2009).

This may be extended to all personal pronouns.

Primary teachers may adapt ratiocination to their students' appropriate developmental level. For example: Code: Red dot. Clue: Stop! Every place you stop when you read… Decode: Put a period (.), an asking mark (?), or an excitement mark (!).

8. Very in my class is considered a four-letter word and as such gets X-ed. But students should understand the rationale behind the X so they may intelligently decode it. As an adverb, very acts as an intensifier for the word it precedes. There's nothing wrong with that, although students often grab very instead of mentally wrestling with precise word choice. To avoid this corroding of precision, students determine if they have used very as an adjective or if they have used it as an adverb. If adjectival, it remains; if adverbial, it tips off imprecision. Students untangle this clue by omitting very and choosing an exact word for its modificand.

9. By the time student reach this clue, they should have had ample work on development by detail, narration, example, illustration, and fact. Coding with two vertical lines encourages close reading to be sure all points have been developed; decoding reminds that more writing is needed.

10. It, clearly a pronoun meant to refer to an idea previously expressed, is often used by students to refer to an idea still in their heads. (How many times have we received compositions beginning with it?) The triangle warns students to examine the referent. If the referent is clear, it remains; if unclear or nonexistent, it must be replaced with something specific, or the sentence must be reworked.

Ratiocination and Revision or Clues in the Written Draft

The Objectives

These clues and decodings

1. enable teachers to integrate lexical, syntactical, rhetorical, and grammatical concepts with composition instruction during the writing process;

2. encourage students to test these concepts immediately in a context that matters to them;

3. provide students with visual ways for reentry into their writing in order to make it better;

4. help students take the responsibility for their own writing;

5. permit students to revise during their process thereby improving their papers before they are handing in for a grade;

6. aid teachers' work evaluating those papers and lightening their paper load.

After all this detective work our class may close as a Carolyn Keene mystery closes. Students discussing this venture will wonder if they'll every have another so thrilling. Assure them they will, perhaps calling the next paper "Secrets of Sentence Beginnings" or "Hidden Word Meanings." And be sure to explain that this, their first paper in a series, should serve as a pleasant reminder of their first solved mystery. Just fiction? Maybe. But maybe not.

Commentary:

Ratiocination is one technique, one strategy, one concrete way teachers have to integrate the teaching of grammar with the teaching of writing during revision. Too many writing projects, too many classrooms, too many writing courses spend too much time on prewriting and not enough time on revision. Ratiocination is the single most effective way 475 teachers surveyed have found to teach revision.

SECTION ONE
Foundations

Chapter One
The Roots of Ratiocination

Setting the Scene

We cannot fault the teaching profession; ever since antiquity countless teachers have been trying to find a way to teach grammar so that students learn it. Constance Weaver in *Teaching Grammar in Context* reaches back in her first chapter to Aristotle and the Stoics when grammar was considered a way to discipline and train the mind, noting that the first grammar text was published in the second century B.C. (3). Carroll and Wilson in *Acts of Teaching* (2nd ed) provide a brief history of grammar beginning with the Greeks and Romans and continuing until today (91-93). Noguchi undertakes "The Paradoxes of Grammar Instruction" in the final chapter of *Grammar and the Teaching of Writing*. And those three references are microscopic to the macroscopic array of books and articles given to the topic.

Grammar Within the Writing Process

Ratiocination, rising up out of the need to teach grammar within the writing process, enjoys a much shorter history than does grammar itself—but its history reveals eight sturdy roots. With such support, ratiocination clearly has tapped the best in rhetoric, educational theory, pedagogy, philosophy, literacy, composition, and grammar, as well as over thirty years of proven success in classrooms.

With one root in American literature, another in the "abstract truth made tangible" balloons of S.W. Clark (Clark, iv), a third in the diagramming techniques of Reed and Kellogg, a fourth in the learning theories of Vygotsky, Bruner, and Emig, a fifth in the learn-by-doing philosophy of John Dewey, a sixth in the sentence combining strategies and generative rhetoric of Strong, Stull, and others, the seventh, a taproot that touches the voluminous amount of brain research, and finally the eighth and oldest root, rhetoric that looks to mastering the process

Grammar Within the Writing Process

of communication, ratiocination provides a solid way into teaching grammar meaningfully while making the act of revising constructive. As A. S. Byatt reminds us, "For many of the new things looked back to very old things for their strength" (132).

Ratiocination's Roots

AMERICAN LITERATURE

While the word *ratiocination* means a reasoning chain of thought, Edgar Allen Poe's fictional character C. Auguste Dupin, considered the first detective of American literature, popularized the word. Using his considerable intellect and his creative imagination, Dupin entered the mind of the criminal, examined the clues, and through the process of reasoning, solved the crime. (See *The Dupin Mysteries and Other Tales of Ratiocination* by Edgar Allan Poe.)

Almost 150 years later, in my seminal article "Ratiocination and Revision or Clues in the Written Draft" (see the Prequel) I drew an analogy between Dupin entering a murder scene to solve the crime and students entering their papers to revise them. Both follow clues, both use logic, both call upon their intellects to reason and make the meaning clearer, both add their creative imaginations to heighten style, and, as is the case with revising, both enter into the minds of the doer. When called upon to revise, neophyte writers often overlook this last but important act. They think a fix here or there will do it, but when more experienced writers go back to revise, they sometimes find their own papers a mystery, so they literally have to fit back into their own minds again. Finally, both use clues to solve the mystery and bring it to a satisfactory close.

THE "BALLOONS" OF S.W. CLARK

Reacting to the monotonous drill and rote memorization of early grammar instruction coupled with the mind-numbing and often confusing exercises of parsing sentences, Stephens Watkins (S.W.) Clark, a creative teacher and principal of Cortland Academy in Homer, New York, believing as Quintillian did that grammar is foundational, devised a "method" in 1847 he believed to be best. "It is confidently believed that the Method of teaching Grammar herein suggested

Chapter One: The Roots of Ratiocination

is the true method" (Clark, iii). Subsequently, his method "revolutionized the teaching of grammar" (Florey, 30).

What Clark did was to compare grammar to geometry and architecture. In other words, Clark believed the learner needed to see the structure; he aimed to make the abstractness of grammar tangible. With that idea as the basis of sentence analysis, he contrived puffy circular and oval constructions, each containing a separate word from a given sentence that billowed relationally on the page. He called these "A System of Diagrams" (Clark, iv). Figure 1.1.

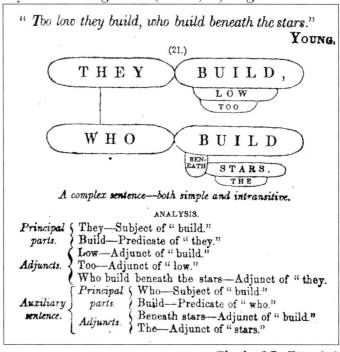

Clark, 35. *Fig. 1.1*

(See *A Practical Grammar: in which Words, Phrases, and Sentences Are Classified According to Their Offices and Their Various Relations to One Another* by S.W. Clark—earliest version 1848.)

My notion of ratiocination, not unlike Clark's method, makes the abstractness of grammar tangible through a system of codes introduced by the teacher and used by the students. These codes enable students to code the clues and then analyze their sentences in ways that help them clarify their meaning and correct any grammatical errors.

The "Ballons" of S. W. Clark

The difference between Clark and my work, though, is this: Clark provided the sentences, whereas I believe students should work with sentences they themselves have written. In that way the sentences hold intrinsic meaning and purpose for them, motivating students to make their writing better.

Like Clark, I have retained the old nomenclature, "not because a better could not be proposed, but because the advantages to be gained would not compensate for the confusion necessarily consequent to such a change" (Clark, iv).

THE DIAGRAMMING OF REED AND KELLOGG

Reed and Kellogg took Clark's bulbous diagrams and flattened them out as a series of lines showing logical succession. Figure 1.2.

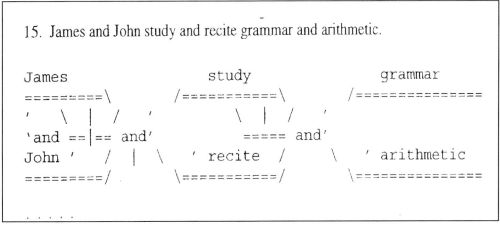

Reed and Kellogg, 50. *Fig. 1.2*

Their stated intent was to "enable the pupil to present directly and vividly to the eye the exact function of every clause in the sentence, of every phrase in the clause, and of every word in the phrase—to picture the complete analysis of the sentence, with principal and subordinate parts in their proper relations" (Reed & Kellogg, 7). Because they believed that students should know the sentence as the skillful engineer knows his engine, they wanted their pictorial diagrams to act as an aid, a map, or picture, "that the pupil can, at a single view, see the sentence as an organic whole made up of many parts performing various functions and standing in various relations" (Reed & Kellogg, 7).

CHAPTER ONE: THE ROOTS OF RATIOCINATION

Ratiocination holds to the same intent as diagramming but again students use their own writing not the writing of skilled authors. Reed and Kellogg cull from works by Ruskin, Thackeray, Hawthorne, Emerson, Holmes, Irving and Lowell, among others, rendering our more contemporary notion of mentor texts a revival of an old technique. Nor does ratiocination invite students "to write up to" some predetermined assignment such as these two examples of another long-endured, old-time method that holds little meaning or interest for students.

> Write the following sentences, using the independent clauses parenthetically:
> 1. We believe that the first printing-press [sic.] in American was set up in Mexico in 1536.
>
> Vary the following sentence so as to illustrate five different kinds of noun clauses:
> 2. Astronomers believe *that stars are suns* (Reed & Kellogg, 118).

These sentences and other like them used by Reed and Kellogg may be structured to invite some modicum of success with the assignment, but because the content of the sentences is either so far removed from the students' experiences or because kids could care less about "using the independent clauses parenthetically," students simply went through the motions.

How much better to teach students the power of the parenthetical, how to craft it to make a point, or how to use it to reinforce or emphasize something in their writing. Merely putting parenthesis around an independent clause is a meaningless assignment if the writer sees no reason for it.

Knowing this, ratiocination insists students re-examine their own writing for its intended meaning, its literary merit, and its logic. While some teachers have turned ratiocination into a mechanical procedure, to be true to the method, students use the color codes then the decodes to come face-to-face with the authentic complexity of *their* writing, compelling them to make decisions at every point.

THE LEARNING THEORIES OF VYGOTSKY, BRUNER, AND EMIG

L. S. Vygotsky

Perhaps ratiocination's roots are buried deepest within the cognitive developmental theory of Lev Vygotsky. For eons, grammar has occupied a narrow place in the English language arts classroom and in education in general. But by tapping the research of this great thinker, we broaden the support of ratiocination as built upon the solid developmental rock of human knowing.

Vygotsky's theories support ratiocination in four areas: play, concept formation, scaffolding, modeling, and collaboration.

PLAY

Vygotsky tells us, "In play a child is always above his average age, above his daily behavior, in play it is as though he were a head taller than himself" (1978, 129). Ratiocination is a type of play. Teachers and often the students themselves are startled by what unfolds from their revising because of this method. After all, it seems as though students are only circling a word or boxing in a phrase, yet something deeply cognitive takes place—the word, the phrase becomes connected to the meaning in a different way—deeper, more thoughtful revision begins. To paraphrase Vygotsky, the student's writing emerges as better, more mature, more interesting, more creative or less formulaic, less typical—in short—"a head taller."

That the coding of ratiocination seems like play is deceiving because coding only initiates the process. It is during the act of decoding, that the writing evolves. The students suddenly see opportunities for semantic and syntactic development and seize upon them; therefore, ratiocination allows students to "play around" with "what ifs" on their way to clarify meaning. As Vygotsky tells it "The relation between thought and word is a living process: thought is born through words." As students look at the word or words they have coded, thoughts form and possibilities present themselves.

CONCEPT FORMATION

"Concept formation is the result of a complex activity in which all the basic

Chapter One: The Roots of Ratiocination

intellectual functions take part" (1962, 58). The journey from unrelated heaps to complexes to pseudo-concepts to genuine concepts parallels the journey students take when applying ratiocination.

First students regard their papers as mere aggregates of words—some in phrases or clauses, most in sentences, but all without any real priority of meaning. Their papers are what Vygotsky would call "unorganized congeries" and there's the problem. How to make these conglomerations meaningful for the reader? So thinking in complexes begins.

Students begin to make subjective connections, that is, connecting what they have coded to *their* meaning, which will and should be different than the connections and meaning of others. And even though the connections are idiosyncratic at this point, students more easily connect after the coding has been done. Then connections rise up out of the pile of words on the page to present themselves for further review. Ratiocination encourages students to look for patterns as the codes invite connectivity. Associations are made, dynamic, consecutive links are forged, and throughout the process, meaning is honed.

Truly, ratiocination sometimes seems to yield dead ends in writing; it seems sometimes to stump students, especially those expecting writing to be as immediate as a text message. Students who think they hit a dead end because they can't think of another way to say something isn't a dead end at all—most of the time it's a pseudo concept on its way to genuine conceptualization. The stumping or the "I don't know if I can do this," is one huge step to becoming successful. The success is not in finding "the answer," but rather in continuing to consider the myriad possibilities when it comes to revising a paper using ratiocination. I call this "rigor" both of mind and method.

My research has shown that with continued "playing around" and application of ratiocination, students' writing moves to a higher standard with students viewing their papers analytically—the parts in relation to how those parts fit together to make a whole, coherent paper. This also allows students to attempt a syntax that may be above or out of their normal register. At first these attempts may sound stilted or academic to the casual language ear, but with continued use, the more sophisticated the syntax and the more rhetorical the writing becomes, the more comfortable students become with difference registers of language. Thus, students begin to understand writing for different audiences and purposes. They also begin to synthesize the entire process conceptually.

The Learning Theories of Vygotsky, Bruner, and Emig

Scaffolding

Nothing in theory lends as much support to scaffold learning than does Vygotsky's ZPD, his zone of proximal development. Vygotsky calls the ZPD "the discrepancy between a child's actual mental age and the level he reaches in solving problems with assistance" (1962, 103). In other words the ZPD is the space between what a learner knows and what a learner can know.

Pulling up learners from where they are to where they can be best happens incrementally, or through what Vygotsky calls "the stages of internalization" (1978, 131). With ratiocination, the process is triply incremental.

- The process of coding and decoding is incremental, beginning with a code, introducing the clues to be coded, and then decoding them.

- Incremental, too, is the gradual introduction of new clues to be coded. Done repeatedly within the students' generated writing, intra class, each concept is soon internalized.

- Finally, the process progresses from class to class. Middle school students build upon what they were taught in elementary school as high school students build upon their middle school learning. Each level becomes more and more sophisticated.

> Several semesters after introducing the code for "to be" verbs in English class, I ran into a former student. After the usual pleasantries, she said in all seriousness and with great respect, "Dr. Carroll, I don't know whether to bless you or curse you."
> Taken by surprise I blurted, "Why is that?"
> "Every time I go to write *is* or *was* my hand shakes!"
> We both chuckled over her kinetic metaphor but we also both knew she had internalized the lesson.

CHAPTER ONE: THE ROOTS OF RATIOCINATION

MODELING

The difference between unassisted performance (telling) and assisted performance (showing)—called *modeling* in educational parlance—is the difference between students operating in a vacuum or seeing the expectations of the lesson. When we talk about modeling, we generally mean the modeling task of the teacher, but following the model is the task of the student.

Vygotsky calls this type of modeling *imitation*, "To imitate, it is necessary to possess the means of stepping from something one knows to something new" (1962, 103). Ratiocination provides those means by showing the students how to code what they know and then giving them the means to step from what they know, what they have coded, to something new—the decode.

Students first watch the teacher apply the code and decode in his or her own writing. Seeing this heightens students awareness of the thought processes, the grappling, the challenge in revision and editing; further, it underscores the power of knowing grammar. Students immediately follow this model by imitating it. They apply the code and decode to their papers. This yin and yang reinforces the interconnectedness and interdependency of teacher/student/lesson and how each gives rise to each other in turn.

COLLABORATION

By now anyone who has studied Vygotsky knows his famous line, "What a child can do in cooperation today he can do alone tomorrow" (1962, 104). This is the essence of collaboration; this gives credence to grouping, conferences, clocking (peer proofreading), teamwork, and any other activity the students work on together.

With ratiocination, although students re-enter their own writing, they also collaborate with peers when they want or need additional input, hit a snag, can't make the revision work, don't understand a grammar concept, or just need another ear. Often a student's knotted sentence goes on a board, chart, overhead, or document camera for collaboration by the entire class.

Jerome Bruner

As we say in *Acts of Teaching (2nd ed)*, "Jerome Bruner has been a major influence in developmental psychology for the past five decades" (257), and he has influenced my work on ratiocination since the late 70s. Bruner's extensive research led him, among other things, "to examine the act of discovery in man's intellectual life" (1971, 82).

Discovery forms the basis of ratiocination for, to paraphrase Bruner, at its core is the rearranging or transforming of evidence to go beyond that evidence to new insights. Holding to Bruner's view that "the student is not a bench-bound listener" but an active participant "manipulating the content of the material by various transformations" (1971, 83), ratiocination calls upon students to consider alternatives and to ask themselves "iffy" questions. After circling a "to be" verb, for example, a student may face three or four active verbs from which to choose a replacement. They may think, *If I choose this one, how will that word affect my meaning? My reader's understanding? Which words best fits my style? I need to look at the sentence before and the sentence following to be sure my revision works in context. How does this influence my progression of thought? My central idea?* Older students may use their circled verbs to illuminate verbals or apposition. Some may be challenged to take four sentences with the same "to be" verb and write all the combinations they can, thereby being exposed to many grammar concepts.

Bruner identifies four benefits of this process: intellectual potency, intrinsic and extrinsic motives, heuristics of discovery, and conservation of memory (1971, 83). We call these the side effects of ratiocination.

Intellectual Potency

Intellectual potency leads to increased cognitive activity—as cognition breeds cognition—which in turn leads to a desire to participate in more discovery. Teachers who share their successes with ratiocination tell us that they often have to stop the students from overdoing the strategy. Once hooked, it seems, the students don't want to stop. They are not content, for example, getting rid of half their "to be" verbs—they want to rid their papers of *all* of them! Noticeably, this more active learning yields higher expectations from both teacher and students.

Chapter One: The Roots of Ratiocination

Intrinsic and extrinsic motives

Extrinsic motives tend to limit the learner. They learn to conform, to learn only what they need for a test, for example, no more. This has a deadening effect in a classroom. When the emphasis is on discovery and intrinsic motives, students feel good about their accomplishments and want to experience that "feel good" sensation again. As students ratiocinate, they experience the intrinsic motivation that comes from knowing learning has occurred, that they have made their papers better, and they know *how* their papers are better; furthermore, they understand how to make future papers better.

Heuristics of discovery

Bruner's heuristics of discovery parallel the philosophy of ratiocination—practice, practice, practice. Like a good basketball team or a person chosen for the Olympics, the heuristics of discovery demand practice at trying to figure things out. Once students apply the code, they practice discovery every time they decode.

Conservation of memory

Bruner's research shows that if students construct their own cognitive processes, what he calls "mediators," for remembering information, rather than using none at all or one given to them by someone else, they make the information more accessible for retrieval" (Carroll & Wilson, 261). When applying conservation of memory to ratiocination, we see nothing *but* students constructing their own cognitive processes. By determining how they will decode, what they will decode, when they will decode, and why they will decode, students literally embed the information into their minds in a way that has staying power.

In addition to Bruner's theories on discovery, his theories about the process of knowing greatly influenced the method of ratiocination. Maintaining that knowing occurs through three modes, Bruner identified the enactive, the iconic, and the symbolic representations of reality as ways to represent reality. All are employed when ratiocinating.

ENACTIVE KNOWING

With enactive or motoric knowing, students learning by doing. The writing hand works the muscles to achieve the desired results. Perfect for ratiocination with its emphasis on students marking up their own papers, getting the feel of what is right, combining sentences, trying new words, fooling with phrases, and evaluating clauses. The hand predominates during this work; Bruner calls this *motor amplification.*

ICONIC KNOWING

Image making, image depicting, image producing, and visualization are all part of iconic or ikonic knowing, which soundly supports the method of ratiocination because in the coding phase graphics play a large role in the process. The eye predominates, so seeing a circle or drawing a box, for example, intensifies the enactive learning. Bruner calls this *sensory amplification.*

SYMBOLIC KNOWING

The third tier of the capacities or amplifications of Bruner is symbolic knowing. Here the knowing comes through language—in this case a restatement of words. The brain predominates. So students move from marking papers in a code, to examining those marks and considering their value, to making meaning, making meaning clearer, or reconstructing the meaning. Bruner calls this knowing *ratiocinative amplification.* That is sound support indeed.

Chapter One: The Roots or Ratiocination

Janet Emig

Besides being a scholar and force in the field of rhetoric and composition, Janet Emig was my major professor during my doctoral studies at Rutgers University and has become mentor and brain mother—by extension—for all the trainers and teachers affiliated with Abydos Learning. As such, Emig has exerted a profound influence upon my work, writing, thinking, and theory. Ratiocination is no exception.

Her article "Writing as a Mode of Learning," which she explained in her interview with my graduate-school colleague Dixie Goswami, "should have a word in the title so as not to mislead—*Analytic* Writing as a Mode of Learning' is what it should be" (122), provided the exact support I needed. When I read, "Writing represents a unique mode of learning—not merely valuable, not merely special, but unique," (123) I realized that ratiocination as revision and editing fits that definition. I realized that when students re-enter their papers to code and decode them, they are learning in unique ways. I realized that all the worksheets, rote, and drill could never match the uniqueness of ratiocination. I realized that the word *analytic* exactly denoted what ratiocination demanded—that students re-examine their own writing in deeply analytic ways to improve their prose, clarify their meaning, and craft their style.

The 2010 Carnegie report, "Writing to Read: Evidence for How Writing Can Improve Reading," which builds on the previous report "Writing Next," examines the impact of writing—in this latest case about reading. Janet Emig's article "Writing as a Mode of Learning" is referenced throughout the report. Therefore, I hypothesize that as part of the writing process, ratiocination, given its emphasis on precision and accuracy, actually may enhance reading:

> This result is consistent with the findings from *Writing Next* that writing about science, math, and other types of information promotes students' learning of the material. In addition, teaching writing not only improves how well students write, as demonstrated in *Writing Next;* it also enhances students' ability to read a text accurately, fluently, and with comprehension. Finally, having students spend more time writing has a positive impact on reading, increasing how well students comprehend texts written by others (Graham and Hebert).

Emig goes on to reference Vygotsky, Luria, and Bruner as examples of "distinguished contemporary psychologists" who hold "that higher cognitive functions, such as analysis and synthesis, seem to develop most fully only with the support system of verbal language—particularly, it seems, of written language." That buttresses ratiocination because "writing uniquely corresponds to powerful learning strategies" (123) and the heuristic of coding clues and decoding them demands that students grab the grammar and wring it out for meaning and style.

THE PHILOSOPHY OF JOHN DEWEY

I don't remember exactly when I realized that John Dewey and I lived at the same time. Of course, he was born earlier, but when he died in 1952 at the age of ninety-two, I was a sophomore in high school. By the time I was a senior in college, I had been exposed to many of his views because one of my major professors, Dr. Adrian, had studied under him. So in some sense I was a contemporary of John Dewey the philosopher, psychologist, and educational reformer and knowing that is humbling.

He wrote copiously, but as undergraduates we did not read all his works. As a matter of fact, I really only remember reading his *Democracy and Education,* most specifically the chapter "Education as Conservative and Progressive." Not a terribly long piece, but most assuredly one that became an adventitious root of ratiocination. Dr. Adrian drilled us in Dewey's technical definition of education: "It is that reconstruction or reorganization of experience which adds to the meaning of experience, and which increases ability to direct the course of subsequent experience" (44). She was adamant about Dewey's distinction between instruction that increases ability and routine or capricious activity.

She believed in sharing the purpose of any assignment with the learner and she believed in learning by doing. What made her unique is that she practiced what she preached. We were not lectured on lessons plans rather we wrote them, taught them, compared them, and assessed them. She did not test us on curricula, but she had us research curricula, even visiting schools as far away as Pennsylvania to see various curricula in action. She did not tell us that we learn by doing, rather she orchestrated the classroom where we were the doers; we were the learners.

This impacted my vision of how grammar should happen within the writing process. Not students memorizing rules or filling in blanks, but students performing

CHAPTER ONE: THE ROOTS OF RATIOCINATION

the work. Hence when students ratiocinate, they code and decode; they, not teachers, mark up their papers to, in Dewey's terms, "reconstruct and reorganize the experience."

But there is another piece, one sometimes ignored by the overworked time-conscious teacher: his notion that "after the act is performed we note results which we had not noted before" (44). Drummed into us was the key of leading students to see the connections between the process and the result. So in working with ratiocination, I remembered that key and knew just coding and decoding were not enough. Reflection had to occur. It became clear as I worked with ratiocination across grade levels (including college) students sharing their results, and teachers debriefing those results helped students see the connections between what they did and what they learned.

SENTENCE COMBINING AND GENERATIVE RHETORIC

William Strong's sentence combining hit the educational scene in the 70s just when I was working on and testing out—ratiocination. William Stull's sentence combining and generative rhetoric came along a decade later while I was still refining my method, roughly one year after my article appeared in *English Journal*. Both bore into ratiocination in powerful ways. Both provided fibrous roots, networks that give ratiocination a strong anchor, roots that preserve the integrity of the method.

From sentence combining I took the notion of students freely "putting together" sentences in new and different ways to improve their writing. After all, sometimes when underlining their sentences in alternate colors, students sat back in shock at all their short choppy sentences. Sometimes with eyes rolling round in their heads they were mesmerized by long, convoluted, out-of-control sentences. They wanted ways to analyze and synthesize them, ways to break them apart or put them together in new and better ways.

From generative rhetoric I took the four principles of style: addition, direction of movement, levels of structure, and texture. What I discovered the year between writing the article that explained the first fruits of my research and reading Stull's book was this: As students became sophisticated in using ratiocination so, too, did their writing gain in sophistication. They not only strove for expanded and greater depth but they yearned to show the richness of their individual style. Stull provided me with a way to help them achieve that.

For example, I introduced three things that build texture: details, attributes, and comparisons (similes, metaphors, thesis/antithesis). When students began coding these, many saw their writing bereft of texture, so they began anew to put it all together.

In short, sentence combining primed the engine for improved writing whereas generative rhetoric provided the steering system to keep that writing moving properly. Both became embedded in ratiocination.

BRAIN RESEARCH MEETS RATIOCINATION

These roots are seminal but voluminous and still growing, reminding me of dendrites themselves. While memory is often unreliable, I think my first interest in the brain and its connection to and with writing came from a fellow classmate, Bud Glassner. While each of us in Emig's doctoral program followed our particular interest—I zoned in on the writing assessments of the students in the project and control groups, Linda Waitkus investigated the dynamic relationship between the poetic and transactional functions in written discourse, Joan Birnbaum followed the reading and writing behaviors of fourth and seventh-grade students, Carmen Collins worked on reading, reflecting, and writing, Alice Brand loved poetry and pursued that venue, while Barbara King Shaver conducted student and teacher attitude surveys about writing—and there were others who fade now from my memory. But the one to whom I owe gratitude for an early root to brain research was Bud Glassner. When we'd seminar he'd dazzle us with his descriptions of the lateral specialization of the modes of discourse he'd discovered; he'd detail his EEG studies at the Rutgers University Medical Center. I was hooked.

After Bud it was an easy step to Roger W. Sperry at California Institute of Technology and his students—Michael Gazzaniga, Jerre Levy and others. Brain research was embryonic at that time but exploding because of new technologies. I devoured Philip Vogel and Joseph Bogen's work on commissurotmies, inhaled Betty Edwards connections of teaching art to new knowledge on the brain, memorized swatches of Robert Ornstein and Richard Thompson's *The Amazing Brain,* read all the Leslie Hart I could find, watched on PBS then read Richard Restak's *The Brain* and all his subsequent books, grappled with Joseph LeDoux's works, especially *Synaptic Self,* and lauded and applauded Caine and Caine, Ramachandran, and Jensen for making brain research accessible to teachers.

How could this explosion of these new insights into that hidden organ locked

CHAPTER ONE: THE ROOTS OF RATIOCINATION

in our skulls not impact my work on ratiocination? Clearly I internalized the brain research, especially about connections and easily found sound support for my method.

Because learning is the primary function of the brain, the principles of brain-based learning fit neatly into ratiocination. While nothing short of an entire book on the connections between how the brain functions and ratiocination would do these roots justice, the following ten points, like a rootstalk that sends out more roots and shoots from its nodes, provide rhizomic support.

MULTI-TASKING

Because the brain does many things simultaneously, no one clue works for every writer every time. Teachers need a repertoire among the many codes and clues to direct the decoding to the grammar skills, revision, and editing needed for particular students. Ratiocination provides that. Nor does one ratiocination technique give a student only one way to revise. Real and deep revision becomes a series of tasks—not right or wrong—but each code presents many possibilities and potentialities. For example, circling "to be" verbs allows changing them to more precise verbs—an exercise in diction—or it may invite a look at the passive construction—an exercise in grammar—or it may demand sentence combining—an exercise in syntax.

LEARNING BEGETS LEARNING

Neurons need nourishment. In truth, learning *becomes* the very nourishment needed by neurons—knowing is the brain's food. As we learn our brains range over something to do, to work with, to feed further upon. Learning moves the learner from a passive recipient to an active doer. We know that challenge and satisfaction affect the brain differently than does threat and boredom. If ratiocination is implemented correctly, there is just the right amount of challenge yielding just the right amount of satisfaction for students of different ages and achievement levels, hence more learning occurs.

PEOPLE MAKE MEANING

In order to create an environment of meaning making, students need novelty, opportunities to discover, choice, yet stability and familiarity. Ratiocination encourages students to re-enter their writing in new and different ways—they are the ones analyzing the writing and marking it up—not the teacher. In experiencing this novel re-entry, students discover many things: new meanings, a chance to change words, the possibility to reformulate whole chunks of their writing, a shot at taking a risk, or an occasion for honing intended meaning.

Revision becomes more sophisticated as the learner becomes more syntactically mature; this constant making of meaning is not a skill learned in first grade and simply mastered, but rather a skill learned, relearned, augmented, and continued throughout a students' writing journey, a skill that depends on the meaning and function of the piece the student ratiocinates. Thus learning always makes meaning, makes new meaning; it becomes a synthesis of what the student reads blended into what the student writes and coupled with ratiocination results in clearer and better writing.

THE BRAIN LOVES PATTERNS

The brain both perceives and creates patterns, making for a major way to learn. Isolated bits of information are so much harder to process than information in patterns. There are many studies that support how appropriate patterning enhances learning—Nummela and Rosengren; Hart; Lakoff; Rosenfield; Russell; Miller to name a few. What ratiocination does for grammar, revising, and editing is present patterns. The patterns of coding, finding clues, and decoding become stimuli for remembering how certain structures work in grammar, how revising isn't just correcting misspellings. After a while students create these patterns in their heads, sometimes even while in the act of writing. (This may also account for some of the original success of Clark's balloons and Reed and Kellogg's diagramming. They offered patterns and those patterns were visual.)

ATTITUDE IS ALL

We cannot deny the emotional side of our knowing. Actually we once separated emotions from cognition—remember Bloom's cognitive taxonomy juxtaposed with his affective taxonomy? With the latest brain research, however, we know both are crucial to learning, so awareness of students' attitudes help or hinder learning.

CHAPTER ONE: THE ROOTS OF RATIOCINATION

With ratiocination, students are expected to know and perfect their grammar; they are expected to revise but not in the usual way. The entire method is new, creating a supportive environment "marked by mutual respect and acceptance" (Caine & Caine, 82).

Both students and teacher understand the complexity involved in revising, in calling upon knowledge of grammar, sentence structure, clarity, coherence, paragraphing, genre, and the rest. So when a student reworks an awkward sentence, for example, the teacher and other students become the sounding board, the listening ear. The teacher is *with* the student not assuming some *I gotcha'* stance. This, in turn, changes the students' attitudes; they want to do better. If they get a pat on their writers' backs for unknotting an awkward sentence, they are more likely to try again. If they get help unknotting that sentence, they are more likely to help others unknot theirs. Frank Smith calls this building learning communities. We call it building solid literacy.

Engaged writers who actively learn how to improve their papers under a teacher who models how to improve them, experience the success of making them better. This experience translates into more positive attitudes than the student who is simply told, "Your writing needs revision." "Edit your paper." Consider what one teacher told me when experiencing ratiocination for the first time. "I remember getting a paper back from a teacher who had written across the top, *REVISE* and thinking *well I would have revised if I had known how.*"

THE CHICKEN OR THE EGG

Does our brain work part to whole or whole to part? Moot question. But it doesn't matter because the brain processes parts and wholes simultaneously. What has become an old saw, "I am a right-brain learner" or "I am a left-brain learner" is tantamount to boiling up that "eye of newt" or "toe of frog." It's scientific superstition. The truth is good instruction supports both because "learning is cumulative and developmental....Parts and wholes are conceptually interactive" (Caine & Caine, 83).

Thus ratiocination happens in the context of the whole—the student's own writing. Students pull out the parts and analyze them in relation to their entire composition, finally examining the whole to see if the parts fit. Additionally, coding and decoding are designed to be cumulative intra class and inter class as students move up the academic ladder. For example, while second graders may code "to be" verbs to check recognition, and fourth graders code them to attempt their hand at livelier verbs, twelfth graders may code them to nudge them in more syntactic maturity. Hence ratiocination is whole to part as well as cumulative and developmental.

Research on grammar for the past 100 years proves that teachers should teach and students should learn grammar in a context. Here is the context. Instead of isolated exercises that may or may be related to the students' writing abilities or interests, ratiocination uses the student's own writing to provide the context for learning the grammar.

"It is the brain that sees; the eyes merely look" (Smith, 47)

Frank Smith sums up an important learning principle. We have known since the 70s that the brain takes in everything—every sound, every movement, every texture, every taste, every aroma—and each stimulus carries with it myriad complexities. For example, hearing a dog bark may make some folks happily remember a puppy they once owned, some may feel the pain of a dog bite, others may conjure an article they read on dog fighting and get nauseous, hearing the barking may nudge some to stop in the pet store, call the vet, or any number of other connections. Ornstein & Thompson tell us in metaphor, "There are perhaps about one hundred billion neurons, or nerve cells, in the brain, and in a single human brain the number of possible interconnections between these cells *is greater than the number of atoms in the universe*" (21).

That single brain fact supports ratiocination. Then there is support based on the visuality of the process; the different colors and the consistency of the colors used; the hand and bodily movements involved as the students code the clues; the coordination between the clues modeled and the eye search for the clues; the lasting image of what is coded, e.g. a circle, box, arrow, and so forth. All of these help the brain respond to the entire sensory environment in which the teaching and learning occurs.

"Is my learning style better than yours?"

Because no one person processes information exactly the same way, "active processing" allows students to make choices and take charge of what they are learning. Once students code the clues, they have myriad ways to go about the

Chapter One: The Roots of Ratiocination

decoding. Ratiocination is not something done to someone else's writing, but gets down to the nitty-gritty of the style and voice of the writer. Choice equals voice with ratiocination allowing for a multiplicity of choice that leads to a powerful writing voice and the development of craft.

Memory—Our Personal Diaries

Tapping our natural memory system is one thing because it does not require any special strategies to kick in, but the memory we call upon for facts and skills is quite another. Ratiocination actually uses the former and enhances the latter because when learning skills that are connected to students' own writing, the learning has a personal context so important for remembering. "Grammar can be learned in process, through stories or writing" (Caine & Caine, 86).

Risk Versus Threat

"Risk is to thinking as vitamins are to nourishment" (Hart 131). Ratiocination is all about giving students brain food, encouraging compositional risks. When students think or say:

I'm going to try saying what I mean another way.

If I move the second independent clause to the front, I wonder what will happen.

Does this word work better than that word?

WOW! I combined two choppy sentences and got a nice long one that sounds better.

When students decode with verve and experience compositional insight, they are taking risks and in the risk-taking their brains reward them with pleasure neurotransmitters such as serotonin and endorphins. "These chemical are key factors in feeling satisfied and rewarded, and therefore in providing motivation" (Ratey, 117).

Conversely, when the brain perceives threat it typically downshifts from the thinking cortex to a more primitive part of the brain where thought is replaced by reaction. Sometimes with mild threats the brain undergoes a back-and-forth process of perception called "irising." As with the iris of a camera, less light enters; there is less perceived and less learned. So in short

Threat: in proportion to perceived threat, downshifting to faster, simpler, and more primitive brain function occurs. As a corollary, the less threat and the more confidence is felt, the more effectively the cortex can be utilized (Hart, 180).

Students rise to the challenge of ratiocination and in turn are motivated by the brain's reward. Consider the opposite—right/wrong worksheets, grammar tests out of context, checklist revision, or editing marks? No challenge, no risk, no reward and little transfer of learning.

RHETORIC

As neuroscientist Joseph LeDoux says, "Learning involves the nurturing of nature" (9). What we are and what we do are shaped by how and what we learn. Ratiocination, a powerful strategy for teaching and applying grammar and deepening the notion of revising, builds upon so many foundational structures, including the sound of words (phonology), the meaning of words (semantics), the grammatical relations between words (syntax), and the students' knowledge about how those words connect to the world (pragmatics). As such, ratiocination is part of rhetoric, itself a word meaning *I say* or *eirõ* in Greek. "Almost anything related to the act of saying something to someone—in speech or in writing—can conceivably fall within the domain of rhetoric as a field of study: phonetics, grammar, the process of cognition, language acquisition, perception, penmanship, social relations, persuasive strategies, stylistics, logic, and so on" (Young, Beck, Pike, 1).

This raises the act of ratiocinating to a linguistic art as well as a linguistic science since it at once embraces the power of thought and how best to convey that thought by placing emphasis on eloquence and form. In other words, to paraphrase Aristotle, it is not what you say but how you say it that counts.

Ratiocination, clearly rooted in the rhetoric of Cicero and Quintilian with its design of invention, arrangement, style, memory, and delivery, goes beyond the oral classical tradition of argument so needed in law courts, political meetings, and ceremonies, to the needs of students in a diverse, global world. The essence of rhetoric, ratiocination is finding, honing, and using the ability to communicate through the written word.

As a process, rhetoric clearly begins with a person's impulse to communicate, to share some experience with others—although this is a somewhat arbitrary starting point since he often has explored his experiences and formulated ordering principles before he feels a desire to communicate. At some stage in the process he must identify his audience and decide what strategy he can use to present his ideas. If he chooses to write rather than speak, he must at some stage begin to write and rewrite what he wants to say. However, the process is not strictly linear, with clearly defined stages; they often overlap—the writing stage, for example, frequently serves as an opportunity to explore and clarify the experience in his own mind. But in spite of this blurring and merging of stages, the writer does at various times shift his attention from his experience and his own resources to his audience and to the written work itself; these shifts of attention constitute the rhetorical process for the writer (Young, Becker, Pike 9).

I Rest My Case

Ratiocination is no gimmick, no cutesy idea born out of some way to keep students busy, no mindless or boring activity, no mere coloring of text, but rather it rises up as a well-documented solid strategy that shifts students' attention from a surface, cosmetic re-entering of a text into a way to augment independent thinking and rigorous writing. This theoretically grounded, this experientially proven, this intramental and deep technique should become part of the writing process of every student at every level.

Chapter Two
Teaching Ratiocination

Fitting Ratiocination into Your Teaching

Setting the Scene

Ratiocination, the scaffold process whereby students code and decode aspects in their compositions, easily allows teachers to teach grammar within the writing process. Further, it promotes deep revision and authentic editing. This chapter offers examples of ratiocination for three different objectives (reporting categories), appropriate for beginning, intermediate, and advanced writers. Each example takes the teacher step-by-step through the process and is grounded in the following ten guidelines. The "Direct Teach" embedded in each example accommodates the basic grammar skill.

DETERMINING WHAT TO RATIOCINATE: TEN GUIDELINES

Because writing involves idiosyncrasies of meaning, style, and purpose, it is difficult to assign a particular grammar concept or an absolute revision technique to a student's work or even to an entire grade. Some struggling writers may need beginning lessons to craft their work while some young children who have been exposed to rich reading and writing since pre-K may be ready for more advanced strategies.

Nevertheless teachers ask me all the time how to determine what to ratiocinate for any paper or sets of papers. I remind them they are professionals and as such make professional decisions. To repeat: These decisions must be based on teacher

Chapter Two: Teaching Ratiocination

objectives (reporting categories), needs of the students, district curriculum, and state and federal standards. Still, guidelines are helpful. Following are ten:

1. **Analyze** the writing of students—this may be an analysis of entire class (What are common or consistent errors among all the students?) or of individual students (What are the errors specific to a particular student?).

2. **Prioritize** mistakes, errors, slip-ups, misconceptions, oversights, typographical errors (for the upper grades or those working on computers), inaccuracies, or if the work is just plain careless or sloppy. Remember to base the priorities on objectives, needs, the district curriculum and standards. For example—*remember* is not on the Dolch high-frequency for first grade and does not appear until the fourth hundred on Fry's *The Reading Teacher's Book of Lists* (3rd ed.) "Instant Word" list, so correcting that word would not get priority over the incorrect formation of the letters h and k in first grade.

3. **Create** an appropriate color code—circles, boxes, brackets, braces, underlines, highlights, etc. Be consistent with colors—red circles, blue boxes, yellow brackets, and so forth.

4. **Model** using a piece of your own writing (preferably), a mentor text, or a student's writing (with permission). Always model, model, model.

5. **Talk** through your process as you model. For example, don't just change a "to be" verb to a more active verb and move on. Rather explain why you made the change or how that change enhances the paper by making it clearer, livelier, or better crafted.

6. **Encourage** students to apply (ratiocinate) the same strategy just modeled using their writing. Monitor by walking around the room and offering help or constructive feedback.

7. **Invite** students to share their "before" and "after" revisions.

8. **Give** plenty of positive feedback, but if a student is off course, work out the revision together or even with the entire class. In a literate climate where the

Ten Guidelines

classroom has become a place for co-operative learning, students will rise to the expectation. This co-operation actually enlivens the class. Don't be satisfied with half-hearted attempts and never accept, "I can't do this."

9. **Consider** ratiocination a positive interactive way to teach grammar and revision within the writing process. On its journey to becoming a better paper, the word *wrong* should be eliminated from all vocabulary. Writing a paper is a learning situation not a "gotcha" situation. Once students realize this, they show their eagerness to improve.

***10. **Most importantly,** DO NOT cover more than one or two concepts per lesson. Ratiocination by its very nature insists upon higher-level thinking. Taking too many concepts at one time may produce "colored papers" or cognitive overload—neither serves the best interests of students.

The Ten Guidelines in Action

To help teachers fit ratiocination into their lessons, I am presenting a series of lessons based on the ten guidelines. These represent different levels with one objective per level as a model. I do not want to mislead anyone into thinking this chosen objective is the only objective that can be used on that level. These are only meant as models.

BEGINNING WRITERS

Grammar Objective (reporting category):
Coordinating Conjunctions

The coordinating conjunction ***and*** lends itself to a series of ratiocination lessons that may take several days and encompasses different grammatical

points that revolve around coordinating conjunctions. These lessons are meant as models. Teachers may follow one or more lessons, picking or choosing based on students' needs, or simply apply the procedure to objectives they wish to address.

STEP ONE

Decide upon a code—a circle, box, underline, etc. In this case these beginning writers used highlighters. (This adds the novelty effect to the strategy because little kids love highlighters.)

STEP TWO

Identify one key grammatical concept from the curriculum—too many at one time results in cognitive overload, becomes coloring, or militates against deeper thinking. Most concepts are complicated and carry many mutations or satellite points, sometimes even ones not anticipated. These beginning writers highlighted the coordinating conjunction ***and***.

STEP THREE

Using a piece of your own writing—not a mentor text because authentic work in progress works better than a finished piece—model by highlighting all the ***ands*** in the writing.

STEP FOUR

Students re-enter their papers highlighting all their ***ands***.

STEP FIVE

That done—the grammar instruction now begins. Occurring in the context of the writing process, direct teach the possible decodes. Never underestimate the power of the direct teach. But telling isn't teaching. The direct teach must be followed by modeling and practice. The old "I, We, They" technique works best. You may try one direct teach a day or just take one for a single piece of writing—the decision depends upon the writing and attention levels of the students.

> **Direct Teach I**
> *And as a Coordinating Conjunction—Definition—Joining Like Things*
>
> Using the writing chosen for step three, point out examples of how **and**, the additive word, joins or connects. Because its name coordinating conjunction has the prefix *co*, show students how **and** joins things that are equal such as two or more naming words or nouns (Mary *and* John), descriptive words or adjectives (bright **and** beautiful **and** talented), action words or verbs (run **and** jump), groups of words such as phrases or clauses (into the school **and** down the stairs).
>
> When I worked with neophyte writers—most struggling with language, I used some sentences from my writing, which I use here, but encourage teachers to choose sentences from their own writing for more spontaneity and authenticity.
>
> We like Dora the Explorer **and** Sponge Bob.
>
> The **and** tells our reader that we like Dora and Bob about the same.
>
> We ate cookies **and** candy.
>
> The **and** tells our reader that we ate two kinds of sweets.

STEP SIX

After modeling, students re-read their papers looking for ***ands*** that join equal things.

CHAPTER TWO: TEACHING RATIOCINATION

STEP SEVEN

Students share the *ands* in their writing that join equal things.

Two examples from young writers:

Maria *and* Jesse play soccer.

The names of two kids who both play soccer are joined by *and*.

My dad says that my dog Skippy is smart *and* cute.

The *and* joins adjectives that describe characteristics of Skippy.

Direct Teach II
When the Coordinating Conjunction **and** *Is and Is Not Needed*

For this lesson, help students understand when *and* is needed and when it is not needed. Write examples on board or document camera. We need the *and* when we write:

Billy **and** Bob came to my party.

Billy and Bob are the names of two people, so the *and* is needed.

We do not need the *and* when we write:

Billybob came to my party.

Billybob is the name of one person, so no *and* is needed.

30

Beginning Writers

REPEAT STEP SIX

Students re-read their papers looking for **ands** that are needed or any that are not needed.

REPEAT STEP SEVEN

Students share the **ands** in their writing that are needed or not needed.

Two examples from ESL learners:

Me **and** Victoria take the same bus.

> The **and** is needed to join the two kids taking the same bus. Here the teacher should note the incorrect use of me in the subject part of the sentence for some future lesson.

RoseMarie is my cousin's name.

No **and** is needed between Rose and Marie because she one person.

Direct Teach III
*Replacing the Coordinating Conjunction **and** with a Comma*

Show students how to replace **and** with a comma. Write on the board or document camera:

We ate cookies **and** candy **and** ice cream **and** chips **and** cake **and** tacos.

Help students see that's too many **ands**. Tell them, "We don't need that many, so we have a neat way to take care of that—we replace the **and** with a comma—that dot with a tail." Together with the students, replace the **ands** with commas.

CHAPTER TWO: TEACHING RATIOCINATION

> We ate cookies, candy, ice cream, chips, cake, tacos.
>
> If students are ready, this would be an apt time to introduce the comma that precedes the last **and** in a series. (We call this the Oxford or Harvard comma.)
>
> We ate cookies, candy, ice cream, chips, cake, **and** tacos.

REPEAT STEP SIX

Students re-read their papers looking for **ands** that may be replaced by commas.

REPEAT STEP SEVEN

Students share the **ands** in their writing that they have replaced with commas.

Two examples from Addy, a young writer:

In dance class we do tap **and** toe **and** hip **and** hop **and** jumps.

Addy said, "That's too many **ands**." So she changed it to:

In dance class we do tap, toe, hip hop, **and** jumps.

Addy added, "We don't need an **and** between hip and hop because hip hop is one dance. I got rid of three **ands**!"

Alex shared his "too many **ands**."

My pets are two dogs **and** one cat **and** one gerbil **and** three fishes.

32

He changed his sentence to read:

My pets are two dogs, one cat, one gerbil, **and** three fishes.

Alex added (in case I missed it), "See, Miss, I put that fancy comma at the end."

Direct Teach IV
The Logic of Things in a Series

Re-introduce the sentence "We ate cookies **and** candy **and** ice cream **and** chips **and** cake **and** tacos" (or one like it). Point out how this sentence illustrates how we often write what pops into our heads in the order it pops into our heads—often with total disregard for logic—the way that makes the most sense or gives us the best order of things. Saying that sets up an opportunity for a lesson on logical sequence. Explain that when we think about the logic of our words, we write clearer so the reader can more easily understand our meaning.

Together with the students re-read the sentence. Invite students to think about the order in which someone would eat those things. Ask if a different order would make more sense. One student suggested:

We ate tacos **and** chips **and** cookies, candy, cake, ice cream.

He reasoned, "People would eat the tacos first because they'd be hot and they'd eat chips with the tacos. Then they'd eat dessert." I wrote his suggestion on the board but continued to nudge students to think about other logical ways to show what was eaten. Following is a progression of offerings from students in March of first grade:

We ate chips, cookies, candy, cake, ice cream, **and** tacos.

Chapter Two: Teaching Ratiocination

The logic the students used here was to join all the C words. Ah! the logic of first graders!

We ate tacos **and** chips **and** cookies **and** candy **and** cake **and** ice cream.

Here the students reasoned that they'd eat the tacos and chips together first, they'd eat the cookies and candy together next, and finally the cake and ice cream, but when they finished someone they noticed they still had a lot of **ands**.

We ate cookies **and** candy, tacos **and** chips, cake **and** ice cream.

These students really worked on what equal things went together and used the comma rule to boot.

We ate tacos with chips, cookies, candy, cake, **and** ice cream.

A few students liked this one because they said they ate the tacos with the chips first, then everything else. They felt good because they eliminated **ands** by telling *how* they ate the tacos **and** chips not just *what* they ate. That apparently triggered an idea because some other students offered:

We ate tacos with chips, cookies, candy, **and** cake with ice cream.

Kids learn from each other or perhaps this proves that patience pays off. Writing and crafting that writing happens slowly—at any level, but especially with struggling or young writers. This last offering won hands down for its logic. The students thought and thought and finally said,

We ate the tacos with chips first, then all afternoon we ate cookies and candy, but the party ended with cake **and** ice cream.

BINGO! Together they came up with a logical, syntactical sentence way beyond the usual writing of first graders. All the modeling, nudging, and revising showed that old ZPD really works.

Beginning Writers

REPEAT STEP SIX

Students re-enter their papers and work with the highlighted ***ands*** and their logic.

REPEAT STEP SEVEN

Students share their papers where they improved their logic.

First grade example:

Michelle wrote

Before

> We had an Author's Tea. **And** we read our books that we wrote **and** drew pictures **and** Mrs. Baker printed them up on the computer. **And** we went on a field trip. We went to the museum **and** the Great Barrier Reef at the theater **and** we went to the park but didn't stay there much. We had a fun time.

After she highlighted all her ***ands***, she changed her sequence for the better. Michelle told me, "It sounds like we did everything in one day, but we didn't, so I changed it."

After

> We had a fun week. One day we made books that we wrote **and** drew pictures **and** Mrs. Baker printed them up on the computer. The next day we had an Author's Tea when we read our books. Wednesday we went on a field trip to the museum. We saw the Great Barrier Reef at the theater. The next day we went to the park but it started to rain so we didn't stay there much. Today I am writing about my fun week.

CHAPTER TWO: TEACHING RATIOCINATION

Most remarkable about this revision is Michelle's opener. After thinking that her writing sounded as if it all took place on one day, she sets up her week. Once she did that the progression of the days of the week formed the foundation for her activities and her logic. Because the students wrote on Friday, the week provided her with a perfect frame. In the rewrite, Michelle also remembers that it rained the day of the park, and that cause/effect detail adds much to her writing. Ratiocination provided Michelle a way to craft and sequence her writing—even in first grade.

Direct Teach V
*Alternatives to the Overuse of **and** at the Beginning of Sentences*

Show students alternatives to the overuse of **and** at the beginning of sentences. Explain that the word **and** is like glue—it sticks one sentence to the other so the sentences make sense to the reader (cohesion), but there are other ways to glue sentences together. When I do this lesson, I teach three other ways to glue sentences together. This may take several days to model.

1. Drop **and** so the sentence begins with the subject, the "doer."

2. Combine or join together two sentences to make one.

3. Repeat a major word from the previous sentence.

Together with the students, I worked with the following authentic piece of primary writing to provide the students with a model. (I have also used this lesson in fifth and seventh grades because starting sentences with **and** is not unique to primary grades. Since then I have been told this lesson works equally well in high school, especially with ESL or ELL students.)

Beginning Writers

He had a balloon. And it popped. And it turned into a lot of balloons. All of his balloons were blue on his birthday. He kept one balloon. And it floated up to Mars. And he saw a space alien and he jumped off of Mars and he went down carefully. And then he poked a needle in it. And he didn't want it any more.

Tell students, "Together let's highlight all the ***ands***."

He had a balloon. **And** it popped. **And** it turned into a lot of balloons. All of his balloons were blue on his birthday. He kept one balloon. **And** it floated up to Mars. **And** he saw a space alien **and** he jumped off of Mars and he went down carefully. **And** then he poked a needle in it. **And** he didn't want it any more.

When I do this, students eagerly want to help me make this writing better. Usually they want to know who "he" is. So we give "he" a name. One group decided upon "Barney."

Then they dropped all the ***ands*** that started sentences. So the piece read:

Barney had a balloon. It popped. It turned into a lot of balloons. All of his balloons were blue on his birthday. He kept one balloon. It floated up to Mars. He saw a space alien and he jumped off of Mars and he went down carefully. Then he poked a needle in it. He didn't want it any more.

The students liked this version much better but wanted to join two sentences together. I asked which two seem to go together. They decided the second and third sentence should be joined, so I wrote both on the overhead.

It popped and turned into a lot of balloons.

Chapter Two: Teaching Ratiocination

When we read it aloud, they sat back, satisfied. So I challenged them further, "Let's see if we need to put Barney's name somewhere else. We have *he* repeated so many times the reader may get lost." They thought it would be best to put *Barney after Mars*, which I did.

Then I furrowed my brow and read "All of his balloons were blue on his birthday." I asked, "Does that fit? Is that good logic?" (I had spent some time priming the pump with the word *logic*.) Do you think this fantasy story happened on Barney's birthday? At this point I counted, "One, two, three—eyes-to-eyes—knees-to-knees," and students turned into a quick conference with their pre-designated partner.

Most dyads opted to simply drop the sentence—the easy way out of the problem. Several pairs were not happy at all with that suggestion. They theorized: When you really think about it, where did that first balloon come from? They wanted something about Barney's birthday to come first. So we worked on that suggestion for a long time, finally agreeing on:

> Barney had a birthday. All of the balloons were blue on his birthday. He held a balloon but it popped and turned into a lot of balloons. He kept one balloon. It floated up to Mars. Barney saw a space alien and he jumped off of Mars and he went down carefully. Then he poked a needle in it. He didn't want it any more.

The most stunning suggestion in this revision was to change *Barney had a balloon* to *Barney held a balloon*.... These students argued that *had* wasn't as clear as *held*. Knowing they were working on diction—word choice—I almost danced around the room. Deciding I had worked those dendrites quite enough, I brought closure to the lesson by asking the students to find the best changes made. There were other lessons lurking here, though, but sometimes it is best not to overkill.

About a week later the teacher sent me copies of her first-graders ratiocinated papers. As you can imagine, the original efforts were riddled with **ands**. Here are three finished pieces:

If I Had a Dolphin

If I could get a dolphin at Sea-Arama, I would have to get a big fish tank at Cliff's Pet Store. I would put my pet dolphin, Marian, in the front yard. Then I would feed it dolphin food. Then I would watch it swim. The End.
And that's the end of my story. Thank you.

—Mary

My dog is small. It has long ears **and** little curls on the bottom of one ear. Its eyes are black but sometimes they look brown. Its mouth is little **and** his lips are black. His teeth are a little sharp. His nose is small, black, always stuffy. My dog is white like snow. He is short **and** skinny **and** skinnier when he takes a bath. When I get home I see him standing up **and** when I try to pick him up he lays down so I could scratch him. Whenever he sees a cat he starts crying **and** barking. I love my dog. His name is Boo-Boo.

—Allen

The Crazy Cat

Once upon a time there was a lady named Sally **and** a man named John. They had a cat named Momo. Now this cat was crazy. All he ever wanted was food. One day they wanted to go to a movie so much that they left the cat with some friends **and** when they got back from the movie their friends would not give the cat back. One night when their friends were in bed they snuck over to their friends' house. They saw Momo tied to a pole. So they untied Momo **and** snuck back home. Now when their friends got up they saw that the cat was gone. They asked John **and** Sally if they had the cat so they said no **and** they lived happily ever after with Momo.

—Amy

Chapter Two: Teaching Ratiocination

I Rest My Case

When I read these compositions, I thought about my first grade writing—a page of ones—and realized yet again how important are high expectations, modeling with authentic writing, scaffolding lessons, and teaching ratiocination. Kids of all ages are capable of writing astonishing stuff.

Just by highlighting **ands**, these beginning writers were exposed to the function of coordinating conjunctions, commas, the Oxford comma, higher-level thinking, choice, *and* at the beginning of the sentence, logic and logical thinking, sequencing, diction, and the realization that there is more than one way to say something. That sure beats mindless worksheets!

Intermediate Writers

Grammar objective (reporting category):
Relative pronouns

I introduced this entire series of lessons by reading *The Day the Relatives Came* by Cynthia Rylant. The novelty hooked the kids and then we have something concrete upon which to hang the concept of relative pronouns.

The relative pronouns—*that, who, whom, whose, which*—enable ratiocination lessons that take several days and encompass many grammatical points. The following lessons are models. Teachers may follow one or more or simply apply the procedure to objectives they wish to address.

Intermediate Writers

STEP ONE

Decide upon a code—a circle, box, underline, etc. In this case we decided to code relative pronouns by <u>underlining</u>.

STEP TWO

Identify one key grammatical concept from the curriculum—too many at one time results in cognitive overload, becomes coloring, or militates against deeper thinking. Most concepts are complicated and carry many mutations or satellite points, sometimes even ones not anticipated. These intermediate writers underlined the relative pronouns <u>*that*</u>, <u>*who*</u>, <u>*whom*</u>, <u>*whose*</u>, <u>*which*</u>.

STEP THREE

Using a piece of your own writing—not a mentor text because authentic work in progress works better than a finished piece—model underlining all the relative pronouns.

STEP FOUR

Students re-enter their papers underlining all their relative pronouns.

STEP FIVE

Here's where grammar instruction occurs in the context of the writing process. Direct teach the possible decodes. You may try one a day or just take one for a single piece of writing—the decision depends upon the writing level of the students.

CHAPTER TWO: TEACHING RATIOCINATION

Direct Teach I
The Function of Relative Pronouns

    Using the writing chosen for step three, show how relative pronouns do two things: introduce a relative clause and connect that relative clause to the independent or main clause.
    Show how a relative pronoun stands in or substitutes for a major word in that main clause, called its antecedent. Spend time showing students how the relative pronoun stands as close as possible to its antecedent. Another way to say this in more kid friendly language might be: Relative pronouns are like relatives—they "relate" in some way to who or what came before them. (This lesson assumes a former ratiocination lesson covered clauses. If not, the first lesson should review clauses and this would become lesson two.) When I modeled this lesson, I used a piece of my writing that compared my sixth birthday party to my cousin Amy's present-day sixth birthday party. The excerpts used here for the lesson came from that longer memoir. It is best, though, if teachers use their own writing.

My friends, **who** were all my age, gave me gifts **that** were carefully chosen.

    In this sentence *who* is a relative pronoun "related" to *friends*. *Who* introduces the unrestrictive (unnecessary) relative dependent clause *who were all my age*. *That* is a relative pronoun "related" to *gifts*. Unlike the *who* clause, the *that* clause is a restrictive (necessary) dependent relative clause *that were carefully chosen* and connects it to the main or independent clause *My friends gave me gifts*.

    I had waxy crayons, **which** held more wax than color, in my pencil box.

    The relative pronoun *which* introduces a nonrestrictive (non essential, almost an aside) relative clause to the main clause *I had waxy crayons in my pencil box*. *Which* "relates" to *waxy crayons*, its antecedent.

Intermediate Writers

STEP SIX

After this modeling, students re-read their papers looking at the relative pronouns they underlined.

STEP SEVEN

Students share the relative pronouns they find in their writing and explain how the relative pronoun connects the relative clause it introduces to the main clause.

Here are two examples from seventh graders:

> In my opinion best friends are special people **who** are there to listen.

> Mari explained how the relative pronoun *who* introduces the relative clause *who are there to listen* to the main clause *In my opinion best friends are special people*. Mari said *who* "related" to *special people*.

> In drill team I am dancing in two dances, **which** I must practice.

> Lisa said that *which* was a relative pronoun introducing a clause that adds more information. Lisa said *which* "related" to *two dances*. I asked why she put a comma before *which* and she told me her computer told her to do that.

Chapter Two: Teaching Ratiocination

Direct Teach II
The Use of the Comma and Relative Pronouns

Help students understand when a comma is used with relative pronouns and when is it not used. Generally we use a comma before *which* but not before *that* and with nonrestrictive relative clauses. The correct practice is to use *that* to introduce a restrictive clause and *which* to introduce a nonrestrictive clause—hence the reason for no comma before *that* but a comma before *which*.

Continuing with my birthday piece, I wrote examples on board, pointing to the *that* and saying, "*That* as a relative pronoun introduces a restrictive or necessary clause and is never preceded by a comma."

I remember Theresa's mother reading aloud a card attached to a five-and-dime store peach ***that*** said something like "for a peach of a girl."

The relative pronoun *that* does not get a comma before it because *that* introduces a restrictive or necessary clause.

Then I said, "But we use a comma before the relative pronoun *which*."

Amy blew out the candles, and the kids were served large pieces of cake, ***which*** they ate but left mounds of icing.

The comma belongs before *which* because the relative clause it introduces is unrestrictive or not necessary *which they ate but left mounds of icing*. While the information is interesting, it is not essential to the meaning of the main clause *Any blew out the candles, and the kids were served large pieces of cake.*

Intermediate Writers

REPEAT STEP SIX

Students re-read their papers looking for relative pronouns that introduce clauses that take a comma and those that do not.

REPEAT STEP SEVEN

Students share the relative clauses in their writing that take a comma and those that do not.

Aladar offered:

> Last night I came home from a basketball game ***that*** made me tired but excited.

> He explained that no comma is needed before *that* because the information is necessary (cause and effect—the game caused the fatigue and excitement) and is therefore restrictive.

Carmella read:

> A boy I have liked for a long time asked me to go to a movie, ***which*** made me think, "It's about time."

> She said the comma is needed before relative pronoun *which* because while the relative clause introduced by *which* shows "my style and craft in writing," it is not necessary to understand the main clause: A boy I have liked for a long time asked me to go to a movie.

At this point I often point out to students that determining whether a relative clause is restrictive and non-restrictive invites some reflection:

> Is the clause necessary to understanding the sentence?

Does the clause add some interesting but not essential information to the main clause.

> **Direct Teach III**
> *The Difference between **that** as a Relative Pronoun and as a Demonstrative Pronoun*
>
> Show students the difference between *that* as a relative pronoun and *that* as a demonstrative pronoun.
>
> We knew the war **that** raged in Europe made life hard. Some of my friends' dads were fighting in **that** war.
>
> In the first sentence *that* is a relative pronoun introducing the restrictive relative clause *that raged in Europe* connecting it to the main clause We knew the war made life hard. The relative clause is restrictive because that information is essential to where the war occurred.
>
> *That* in the second sentence simply points out something. Demonstrative pronouns point out someone, some place, or something that was already named. *That* points out a particular war. In this sentence, *that* is singular but because it points to a war at a distance so *that* not *this* is used.

Repeat Step Six

Students re-read their papers deciding if their *thats* are relative or demonstrative pronouns.

Repeat Step Seven

Students share the *thats* in their writing explaining if they are demonstrative or relative pronouns.

Intermediate Writers

José, who rarely contributes, surprised us with:

My parents had a fight last night. I wanted to tell my girl friend about **that**.

José said, "I never understood demonstrative pronouns, but I do now. My *that* points to the fight my parents had. Since it happened the night before, I used *that* not *this*."

Doree followed José. She also wrote about confrontation:

He said he needed to talk but **that** wasn't what I wanted.

Doree said her that was a relative pronoun. It introduces the relative clause **that** *wasn't what I wanted* and connects it to talk.

Direct Teach IV
The Difference between Relative Pronouns and Interrogative Pronouns

Show students the difference between relative pronouns and interrogative pronouns. Students usually know the interrogative pronouns, but don't commit "assumicide"; review them. The five interrogative pronouns are *who? what? which? whom? whose?* Aside from *what*, students see immediately that the words are the same for both relative and interrogative pronouns.

The big concept for students to wrap their brains around is this: Relative pronouns may be found in a question but interrogative pronouns are always found in a question. Write a sentence or two on the board as models. Begin with something easy.

Who is coming to Amy's party?

Chapter Two: Teaching Ratiocination

> Clearly *who* is an interrogative pronoun. Not so clear is whether the who in this next sentence is interrogative or relative:
>
> All her classmates and anyone else **who** is part of her life now? I probed.
>
> Some students reason that if you extract *Who is part of her life now* it could clearly be asking a question. But when this came up in the lesson I explained that is why we have to examine grammar in a context. In this context *who* relates to *anyone else* and is therefore a relative pronoun. That it happens to be in a question does not automatically make it an interrogative pronoun. (Some textbooks explain it by saying it is an interrogative pronoun used as a relative pronoun since it introduces a relative clause, but explanation without context is a bit like a banana split without the banana.)

REPEAT STEP SIX

Students re-read their papers deciding if their pronouns are relative or interrogative.

REPEAT STEP SEVEN

Students share the pronouns in their writing explaining if they are relative or interrogative.

Here are two eighth-grade examples—both from Fred.

After our argument, BJ thought he was so cool when he asked, "**Which** of these is yours?"

Fred identified *which* as an interrogative pronoun.

Janet stared icicles at BJ. She knew the answer but she didn't want him to know, **which** is what happened.

Intermediate Writers

Fred said here *which* was a relative pronoun. He reasoned that *which* introduces the nonrestrictive relative clause *which is what happened* and connects it to the first part of the sentence.

Direct Teach V
Crafting Writing Using Relative Pronouns

In crafting writing, if students know how to use relative pronouns they can choose to keep some sentences short or they can connect or insert a relative clause to achieve the effect of smoother discourse.

I used the following couple of sentences from my writing as the model. Teachers are best served if they use their own writing as models. The original read:

Even as we partied our car sat on cinder blocks. It waited for the war to end.

Before we started revising, I thought it important to raise the issue of author's intent and style versus strict usage. So I asked, "Why would the author say the car was waiting for the war to end? Can cars wait or do people wait?"

The students were quick to point out the figurative language of personification. "That's it? That simple?" I asked. They pondered. Finally one of the boys said (I thought quite eloquently), "Cars are like their owners. Like when I was about four I had one of those plastic cars and loved it. It could go faster than my toddler legs—I thought of it as a part of me. I think now when I read about cars or motorcycles they are like extensions of people. So the author probably did the same. That would be you, right, Miss? Do you think of cars like that?"

"Do you mean, do I think of cars figuratively?"

"Yeah, like symbols for people. Here you say the kids are having a party but the car can't move. Seems like the car represents all the people during the war who couldn't move."

Sylvia jumped in. "My dad calls our car by a name—like it's a person."

"Do you think your dad is thinking figuratively when he does that?"

"Maybe."

Myrna asked, "Why was it on cinder blocks in the first place?"

Jacob quipped, "No tires."

I explained the situation during World War II, the shortages of things like rubber that went, as we said then, "to the war effort." The kids found that fascinating, but I pulled them back to the lesson. "Let's tackle these two sentences with all that in mind and see what happens. Keeping style in mind can be important in revision and editing, so I am glad you care about my style." So we fooled around with relative pronouns and came up with these options:

   a. Even as we partied, our car, **which** was tireless and on cinder blocks, waited for the war to end.
   b. Even as we partied, our car **that** no longer wore tires sat on cinder blocks waited for the war to end.
   c. Even as we partied, our car, **which** had no tires, sat on cinder blocks waiting for the war to end.
   d. Our car, **which** had no tires and sat on cinder blocks, waited for the war to end even as we partied.

Thinking of test situations, we debated which option was best.

- Some chose *a* because they could easily identify *which* as the relative pronoun introducing the unrestrictive relative clause.
- Others thought *b* sounded awkward but recognized *that* as introducing the relative non-restrictive clause. Others liked *b* because of its figurative language and the image of the car wearing tires and waiting for the war to end.
- About one-third of the class didn't like *c* because they thought "which had no tires" was wordier than the word *tireless* in *a*. This prompted one student to make another case for *tireless* as a multi-meaning word. Probably a kid bound for the law school, he asked, "Is the car not tired as in not exhausted or is the car without its tires? I think c is the best because it says what it means." Good point. A few students argued with him, though, holding that tireless made the sentence more interesting, especially in light of the war.
- Most didn't like *d* because they didn't like the adverbial clause at the end of the sentence.

The kids then discussed *a* versus *c*, but ultimately decided on *c*, which they didn't like at first but were persuaded to choose by our budding barrister.

Following this model, the students re-entered their papers to see what they could do with relative pronouns and relative clauses.

I saved two before and after eighth-grade examples:

Before:

He really went irate and radical. When he started to have an attitude I said, "Well, what about you ignoring me Sunday?"

Chapter Two: Teaching Ratiocination

After:

He really went irate and radical, which made me become irate and radical, so I said, "Well, what about you ignoring me Sunday?"

Nice parallel structure achieved in the revision. Also, this revision clarifies tone and meaning.

Before:

Best friends stand by your side always. They make you feel better when you're really down.

After:

Best friends always stand by your side, which makes you feel better when you're really down.

Tighter, better writing resulted from this revision. The adverb *always* enjoys its rightful place beside stand rather than beside side.

As closure for this bout of ratiocination, I set up an anchor chart with the prompt: "What did you learn?" Following are some of responses:

- relative pronouns
- that and which
- how a relative pronoun introduces a relative clause
- a relative clause
- I like thinking of them as relatives
- interrogative pronouns
- you can say stuff different ways
- cool commas, like when to use them or not
- I didn't know what a demonstrative pronoun was until today
- a new way to combine sentences—instead of and or but
- figurative language—style
- tone

I Rest My Case

Using a classic picture book—*The Day the Relatives Came* by Cynthia Rylant—to teach a difficult grammatical concept—relative pronouns—helped students make connections. As with so many mentor texts, some allow direct modeling while others such as Rylant's book, offer an effective way to scaffold the teaching and learning experiences so the knowing emerges. These intermediate writers now control a repertoire for crafting their writing because they understand through their own writing the power of relative pronouns and clauses. It's a two for one deal—they improve their writing as they increase their knowledge of grammar and revision.

Chapter Two: Teaching Ratiocination

Advanced Writers

Grammar objective (reporting category):
Verbals

Among the major grammar concepts for those more advanced writers at any age but particularly in high school—are verbals (infinitives, gerunds, participles). This entire ratiocination lesson takes several days and encompasses many grammatical points.

Step One

Decide upon a code—a circle, box, underline, etc. In this case we coded verbals by bracketing [ ].

Step Two

Identify one key grammatical concept from your curriculum—too many at one time results in cognitive overload, becomes coloring, or militates against deeper thinking. Most concepts are complicated and carry many mutations or satellite points, sometimes even ones not anticipated. I decided to begin with the easiest of the verbals—infinitive phrases. These advanced writers began by bracketing all infinitive phrases.

Step Three

Using a piece of your own writing—not a mentor text because authentic work in progress works better than a finished piece—model bracketing all the infinitive phrases.

Step Four

Students re-enter their papers bracketing all the infinitive phrases.

Advanced Writers

STEP FIVE

Here's where grammar instruction occurs in the context of the writing process. Direct teach the possible decodes. You may try one a day or just take one for a single piece of writing—the decision depends upon the writing level of the students.

Direct Teach I
Reviewing Verbals—Emphasizing Infinitive Phrases

First I reviewed verbals, concentrating on infinitive phrases. I showed how we form the infinitive with *to* plus the base form of a verb—*to work, to make* an infinitive phrase.

Working with advanced kids who loved writing enabled me to model for them and the teachers by using a prewriting piece of my own writing. I placed it on the document camera and invited the class to help me bracket the infinitive phrases.

I used a short piece of my writing entitled:

Planting Buttons

In the days of ration books and paper drives, when everything went to the war effort and everything was scarce—even crayons, we had Mom's treasured button box. She'd turn the frayed collars of dresses and change the buttons for a new look, but she always let us play with the buttons. We'd use string [to contrive] spinning tricks with those buttons, we'd make them dance, we'd heap them, line them up, or pretend they were characters from the stories Mom read us. But one day, bored with all that, I said to my little sister, "Edie, let's go outside and plant the buttons." She always agreed, too young not [to…]. So with Mom in the basement washing clothes, out to the Victory Garden we toddled. Planting looked like fun. When Mom did it, she hummed and smiled.

> Pull out a carrot, put in a button—all along the rows we went.
>
> Suddenly Mom flew out of the house, "What are you kids doing?" she called.
> "Planting your buttons," I replied.
> "What? Why?"
> "So you'd have new ones."
>
> She plunked down on the last step, head in hands laughing and crying simultaneously but calling us to her.
>
> We snuggled into her arms and waited. We waited for the buttons [to grow]. We waited for the war [to end]. We waited for our daddy [to come] home.
>
>   We began by bracketing the obvious phrases: to contrive, to grow, to end, to come.
>   Several students suggested *to the war effort* and *to my little sister, to the Victory Garden,* which provided the teachable moment for the difference between infinitive phrases and prepositional phrases. (If a verb follows *to*, it's an infinitive phrase; if a noun or pronoun follows *to*, it's a prepositional phrase.)
>   One student questioned *too young not to*. Again, as is always the case when teaching grammar within the writing process, the opportunity presented itself to discuss style. Then we talked about what was inferred in *too young not to*—what? The students were quick to answer "Too young not to agree." So they concluded that was an implicit—not stated—infinitive phrase.
>   This points out the power of teaching grammar in context. We didn't even get to the decoding yet students were exposed to three grammar concepts:
>
> - identifying infinitive phrases
> - seeing the difference between infinitive phrases and prepositional phrases
> - understanding that inference may occur in grammar

With the infinitive phrases bracketed, we began to decode.
Is each bracketed infinitive phrase necessary or not necessary?
Is there another way that better expresses our meaning?
Could we move or rearrange the infinitive phrases to add emphasis or more power to our writing?

These students concluded that *to contrive* is necessary but they decided to move it to the beginning of the sentence for variety of sentence beginning. Once they did that, they saw how I had lost parallel structure, so they corrected that. The sentence then read:

To contrive spinning tricks with those buttons, we'd use string, make them dance, heap them, line them up, or pretend they were characters from the stories Mom read us.

Several students expressed dissatisfaction with that redo, so they tried again:

To contrive spinning tricks with those buttons, we used string. We made them dance, heaped them, lined them up, or pretended they were characters from the stories Mom read us.

Everyone liked the sound of the second revision, so I asked what we had done grammatically to achieve that. Silence. I asked what words *we'd* contracted in the first revision. Someone suggested *we had* but when we read it as *we had use string*, it didn't make sense. Finally, someone said *we would*, which made sense. So the question remained, what did we do? Here is a sampling of their responses:

- we moved *to contrive* to the beginning of the sentence
- we made *to contrive* part of a long introductory phrase by joining the infinitive phrase with a prepositional phrase
- we turned the one long sentence into two sentences

Chapter Two: Teaching Ratiocination

> - we changed *we'd* to the simple past tense
> - we used parallel structure for the second sentence. I was pleased.
>
> As for *to grow, to end, to come* they thought they should remain but needed to be rearranged in what they considered a more chronological order, considering the word *end* as a great way to "end" the story. They also pointed out—and kids always impress and astonish me—that "daddy" last sounded more like the war might end and daddy still wouldn't be home. They thought that order inferred "daddy" wouldn't ever come home. *Good point*, I thought. Our final revision read:
>
> We waited for the buttons to grow. We waited for our daddy to come home. We waited for the war to end.

We followed the same procedure for the gerunds and participles.

I Rest My Case

I love Anne Lamott's *Bird by Bird*. It captures a family anecdote about her brother. Assigned a report on birds, he typically—in ten-year-old fashion—procrastinates until the night before. With books on birds spread out before him, he froze until on the verge of tears. Lamott's father sat down, put his arm around the boy's shoulder and said, "Bird by bird, Buddy. Just take it bird by bird."

Verbals, indeed every grammatical concept, need to be taken "bird by bird." Only with patience and the metaphoric arm around the shoulder will students begin to understand these abstract concepts. Ratiocination provides both the scaffold and the reassuring arm.

These ratiocination lessons demonstrate how easily a concept may be extracted from the curriculum to be taught within the writing process. The simple scaffold of coding the "clue," which is essentially the concept, and then teaching that concept while decoding makes grammar, revision, and editing within the students' writing palatable, challenging, yet rigorous brain fun.

Section Two
Mentoring Lessons

Section Two: Mentoring Lessons

Setting the Scene

While there were many lessons presented in Section One, Chapter Two, they were meant to show how to teach ratiocination using different objectives. There I followed the ten guidelines. The lessons suggested in this section have a different purpose, they are meant to show how ratiocination may be geared to specific grammar skills and revision levels: emergent, transitional, medial, and advanced. In other words there may be transitional revisers in fourth, seventh, tenth, or even twelfth grades. The level depends upon the writing experiences of the students, not upon their grade levels nor even stated objectives. These lessons follow a broader, more general approach. Hopefully, by juxtaposing several approaches, teachers will find a comfort zone that fits their own personal teaching styles and the needs of their students.

Teaching and using ratiocination takes work, hard work on the part of teacher and students. Teachers must be knowledgeable and willing to plan, model using their own writing, and be prepared for all the idiosyncrasies of language. Students must be willing to re-enter their writing to make it better, think through to their meaning, manipulate language, and take risks.

Chapter Three
Emergent Revision
Shawn and Jon

Emergent revision, while usually associated with the primary grades, often marks the emergent writer in the English language or students who have had few authentic writing experiences along their educational journey. Bred on worksheets or formula or writing in another language, the writing of older students may show some characteristics of a young or tentative writer.

With that caveat in mind, let's look at a typical kindergartener's piece of writing to see if we introduce ratiocination we could tap most of the expected standards.

MENTORING LESSON ONE:
BEGINNING SENTENCES WITH UPPER CASE LETTERS AND ENDING WITH TERMINAL PUNCTUATION.

This piece came from Shawn. (Fig 3.1) One of the first pieces in his journal, under a picture he drew of a long building with windows with a bird or flower in one window, it read

> my Father cot a prtr
> he Fut it in the grenhs

The teacher wrote, "What did your father do with the partridge he caught in the greenhouse, Shawn?" To which Sawn replied

> We lat it go

Chapter Three: Emergent Revision

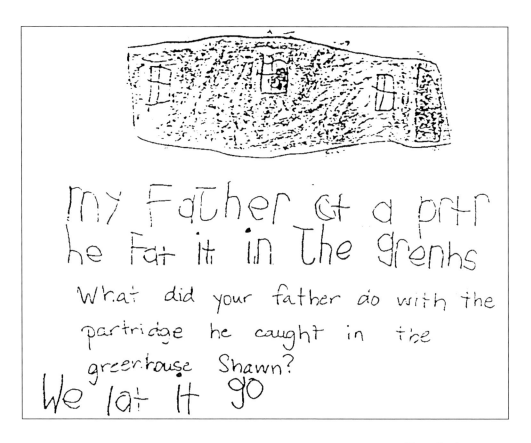

Fig. 3. 1

We see that Shawn is phonologically aware and uses his knowledge of phonics as he writes. We also see that when the teacher responds, she uses the same words he used, which she spells correctly as a model. We also see Shawn knows upper-case letters, applying that knowledge to the word *father*, which he capitalizes because it is important. Following the logic of a five-year-old, we see that Shawn also capitalized *put*, spelled *fut* perhaps because he thought it began with the same letter as *father* or perhaps because without front teeth, that is the sound he hears. Still Shawn knows the *p* sound as he used it correctly as the initial sound of *partridge*. Shawn also knows the compound word *greenhouse*.

So what shall I have Shawn ratiocinate?

    Me: I like your writing, Shawn. I especially like how you illustrated your story. Will you read it aloud to me?

Shawn read his story with ease and clarity. He conveyed a sense of pride as he read.

    Me: We are going to do something with this great piece of writing. We are going to make it even better. Would you like that?"

    Shawn: Yes and my father would too.

    Me: Good, let's get busy.

One of the major concepts in kindergarten writing, one found in all the standards, is beginning a sentence with a capital and ending it with a terminal mark—the emergent signal of beginning sentence sense. Because Shawn is adept at writing simple sentences—he has three—I asked him to put a green circle around the first word in each sentence and a big red dot at the end of the sentence as I read each sentence.

We did this together as the other students watched. Shawn became my model.

    I read: My father caught a partridge.

Shawn put a green circle around *my* and a huge red dot after *partridge*.

    I read: He put it in the greenhouse.

Shawn circled *he* and made a big red do after *greenhouse*.

    I read: We let it go

CHAPTER THREE: EMERGENT REVISION

Shawn circled *We* and put the red dot after *go*.

So that quickly and easily Shawn coded his paper. Now it was time to decode by direct teaching, modeling, and giving Shawn the opportunity to apply the decoding. It went like this:

Me: Shawn, when you ride in a car or on the bus, do you notice times when the driver stops?

Shawn: He stops at stop signs and when the light is red.

Me: Exactly. Red is the color that says or signals "stop." So why do you think I asked you to put a big red dot at the end of your sentence?

Shawn: So I'd stop.

Me: Yes, and even more importantly to signal your reader to stop. Otherwise your reader may just keep reading and get all mixed up with the words. So let's take our pencil and put a small dot at the end of each sentence.

Shawn: OK.

Me: Did you ever notice other marks at the end of sentences? I showed Shawn a book with question marks and exclamation points.

Shawn: (pointing) That one means asking and that other one is an excitement mark.

Me: Great observation, Shawn. You could be a detective. Could we put either one of those marks anywhere in your writing?

Shawn: (Re-reading and after much thinking) After *go*

Mentoring Lesson One

	'cause that was the exciting part. He like stumbled and flapped before he flew. We were cheering him.
Me:	Gee, Shawn, that would be neat information to add to your story. You might think about doing that.
Shawn:	It won't fit.
Me:	Don't worry; I'll give you more paper. Now let's look at those green circles. Do they remind you of anything?
Shawn:	Red light/green light.
Me:	What happens when the red light turns green?
Shawn:	You go.
Me:	That's another signal for your reader. That tells the reader your sentence is beginning, so we put a capital or upper-case letter on the first word of a sentence to send that signal. Isn't that cool? See, you can see how that works in this book.
Shawn:	I did it once.
Me:	Yes, you did. You capitalized *We* in your last sentence. Now go back and capitalize the other first letters.

That was all I did for that lesson. Following this model, the other students marked their papers with their red and green crayons with the teacher and I assisting.

Chapter Three: Emergent Revision

What did we learn from Shawn's ratiocinating?

- transcribing spoken words into print to communicate
- recognizing the difference between a letter (the first letter in the first word of a sentence) and a word
- capitalization
- terminal punctuation
- following oral directions
- using mentor texts
- sharing writing with others
- the possibility of adding text
- revising/editing
- upper-case and lower-case letters
- past tense
- answering a question in writing

Often with students emerging into authentic writing, we find run-on sentences, comma splices, fused sentences, no capital letters, no terminal marks—just word after word after word with no promise anywhere of sentence sense. Often this lack of where a thought begins or ends tells us we are working with an emergent writer, a student—whatever the age—who needs modeling and mentor texts to use for imitative understanding of these essential concepts. Like Shawn, these students may have some phonological awareness, some rudimentary knowledge about writing but their lack of experience with the written word places them in this emergent category.

Mentoring Lesson Two: The OU Vowel Sound

Students who are encouraged to write what is on their minds and in their heads at a young age actually fall in love with the act of ratiocinating—but older students do, too. They blossom under the mastery it gives them over their writing; they adore all the colors, but mostly they like the "figuring it out." The brain loves a challenge after all.

This sample (Fig 3.2) came from Jon soon after I visited his class in early

Mentoring Lesson Two

November. The teacher used "story paper," that horrid paper that leaves a space at the top of the page for the drawing and then gives several lines for writing. Students typically stop when the lines end. I believe in giving students lots of paper, big paper for the emergent writer. They will fill it.

Jon used the blank area for his symbolic representation of the sun shining on a cage of chicks apparently at the farm. A strange round figure sits beside it that may or may not be an insect or an arachnid. Under the illustration Jon wrote this letter to me:

Dear Dr. Carroll,

I remimber wen you came to are class. And we got in gropos and studed about insects and aractneds. Plus we hatched. − 17 egg and some pepal got to tahe 1 chich home and I was one of them. We tohe hem to a farm and his name was Albert. love Jon

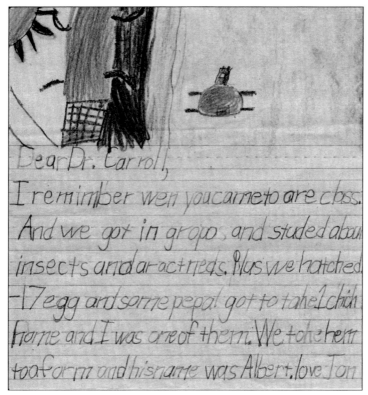

Fig. 3.2

CHAPTER THREE: EMERGENT REVISION

Jon is, of course, applying his knowledge of letter writing in this piece of discourse. He knows the correct salutation (followed by a comma no less), closing, and signature, which he wrote on the same last line as his text because it was the last line on the paper.

We see that Jon usually applies his phonics (although he still mixes his *h* and *k*), knows sentences, refrains from too many *ands*, supplementing one with the transitional word *plus*, which adds coherence to his letter. He capitalizes my title and name as well as *Albert's, I*, and the first letter of the first word in a sentence. He is clear on terminal punctuation and spells many but not all high frequency words correctly. He published his letter by sending it to me.

So what shall I have Jon ratiocinate? I decided upon the *ou* vowel sound, the diphthong in the word *our* contrasted with the *ar* vowel sound in the word *are*. This is a common mistake made by young writers, sloppy writers, or ESL and ELLs. Also, I wanted to address Jon's apparent confusion between the letter *h* and the letter *k*. I worked with Jon individually while the other students engaged in workshop with their teacher monitoring them.

Me: Jon, I like the letter you sent me very much. I can see you took time with your illustration and with your writing. I especially like how you remembered not to begin every sentence with *and*.

Jon: Thanks. I did work hard. Can you see I had a small *p* for *plus* but erased it to make it capital?

Me: Yes indeed, Jon. That was so smart of you. Would you like to see another place or two where you could change something to show how smart you are?

Jon: Yes.

Me: First, could you read me your letter? I would also like to hear it in your voice.

Mentoring Lesson Two

Jon stands and directly faces me, reading his letter to me in a loud, clear voice.

Me: Thank you, Jon. Good job. Let's play detective and look for clues in your letter. Would you like that?

Jon: Sure.

Me: Let's circle a few words in your letter. They will be our clues. OK?

Jon: Sure.

Me: What are your favorite colors?

Jon: Red and blue.

Me: OK. Let's circle *are* in red. Then let's circle *tahe*, *chich*, and *toke* in blue.

Jon: Gotcha. (Jon proceeds to circle the words in the appropriate colors.)

Me: When you read your letter, Jon, you pronounced *our* like *are*, so that's the way you spelled it in your letter. See (showing him on a chart and pointing to the word in his letter), *our* is the word you want not *are*. When o and u run together in a word, they sometimes say the sound *OW* as if they were pinched. (I say the word exaggerating the *ou* diphthong.) Now you say it, Jon. (He does.) Say these other words with *ou* that sounds like *OW*, Jon. (I write them on the chart as I say them; Jon repeats them.) These *ou OW* sound all happen at the beginning of the word: *out, our, ounce, ourselves, outdoors, ouch, outline, outside, out-*

69

Chapter Three: Emergent Revision

look, outcry, outfield.

But sometimes the *ou* runs together in the middle of a word like *hour, sound, about, around, round, scout, aloud, loud, found, cloud, count, house.* (Here I repeat the procedure from above.) Guess what, Jon, there is one word that ends with that *ou OW* sound. It is an old time word *thou.* Got it, Jon?

Jon: OW! (pretending to pinch himself)

Me: You make me laugh, Jon. That was a funny joke. Now let's look at *are*, the word you wrote. You make the *ar* by first saying *ah, ah, ah* then *ar.*

Following the procedure above Jon and I practice the *ar* sound in the initial, medial, and final position with these words:
 initial: *are, arm, army, art, artist, ark*
 medial: *card, March, farm, hard, part, large, garden, start, dark, yard, party*
 final: *car, far, bar, jar, tar, scar, star*

Me: Now let's look at your letter. Do you want *are* class or *our* class?

Jon: It needs to be *our.*

Me: Good thinking, Jon. Let's make that change like you make the lower-case *p* change. (After giving Jon time to make the change.) Are you ready for more, Jon?

Jon: Sure.

Me: Look at these words in your letter that you circled in blue: *tahe, chich, tohe.* Let's read the two sen-

tences with those words.

Jon reads *take*, *chick*, and *took*.

> Me: Hmmmmmm.
> Jon: What?

> Me: Well, Jon, you read those words correctly, but it looks like you get the letters *h* and *k* mixed up. Do you? (Jon looks puzzled.) Here's how we make the letter *h* and here's how we make the letter *k*. The *h* sound is more like breathing but that *k*, well it sounds like a *kick*—*k, k, k*. You lift the back of your tongue for a moment to stop the air and then release it. (I say the sound and Jon repeats it.) Jon, when I was a little girl there was a song called *K-K-K-*(say the sounds of *k* not the name of the letter) *Katy*. It went something like this:

K-K-K-Katy, K-K-K-Katy,
You're the only g-g-g-girl that I adore;
When the m-m-m-moon shines,
Over the cowshed,
I'll be waiting at the k-k-k-kitchen door.

> Jon: Oh, yeah. (Jon was not a bit impressed with my song!) I make them the same. He immediately changes the *h*'s to *k*'s.

> Me: Now let's look again at *take* and *toke*. You have *take* correct when you made your *k* correctly. So that clue helped you see you made a good change.

> Me: But you wrote *toke* not *took*. *Took* has two *o*'s that carry a short *oo* sound as in words such as

CHAPTER THREE: EMERGENT REVISION

> *look, good, hook, afoot, hood, wood, cookie, wool, brook.*

Jon makes the change.

WHAT DID WE LEARN FROM JON'S RATIOCINATING?

- the transitional word *plus*
- capitalizing the first letter of the first word of a sentence
- reinforcing the concept of capitalizing proper names
- capitalizing the letter *I* when it stands alone
- ideas in chronological order
- reinforcing complete sentences and terminal marks
- subject/verb agreement
- the high frequency work *took*
- sharing writing
- publishing writing
- the formation of the letters *h* and *k*
- the *ou* diphthong
- the *k* sound
- the *h* sound
- the short *oo* sound

Just as young writers hear words differently, so do many older students. When we read their writing, we think they are semi-literate or poor students when it may simply come down to a quick phonics lesson.

Chapter Four
Transitional Revision Moving from Imitative to Cognitive Understanding of Grammar
Amanda and Mariana

Flexing their young writing muscles, transitional revisionists range all over the place when writing. Some days they focus, writing interesting, well-constructed stories whereas other days they tell boring bed-to-bed stories replete with disjointed details. Still, if students love to write—more often than not filling pages and pages of text—they love sharing what they have written.

In the sample I have chosen, we see how awesome transitional writers can be, especially when consistently exposed to mentor texts—in this case fables. Amanda proves the power of modeled mentor texts, reading good literature, and teachers who encourage students to develop their own writing voices.

I chose Amanda's five-page book (Fig. 4.1), written early in the year.

page one (title page) (Fig. 4.1.1)

The Lion And The Tiger.

(Below the title Amanda drew a delightful lion facing a darling tiger.)

by Amanda

Chapter Four: Transitional Revision

page two (Fig. 4.1.2)

> Once opon a time there was a lion.
> The lion was very very sick. He lie in bed moning and groaning.
> Well the tiger herd this. And went to the lion. And said. What is wrong?
> The loin said. I'm sick. Oh, I wish I was not a lion! The tiger said. That's the wrong adatude! You should be very happy your a lion!

(Below the text we find the lion sprawled out on a bed with a concerned tiger at the foot of the bed. To the far right Amanda symbolically represented an elephant, mouse, cat, monkey in seven cages piled atop one another with two stick-figure figures—one a girl, one a boy—at the bottom of the cages.)

page three (Fig. 4.1.3)

> The lion said. I geass your right!
> The tiger gave the loin some pills. And right when he swallowed the pills he was better!

(Now we find the bed empty with the head of the lion and the entire tiger saying Ya! in two conversation bubbles.)

page four (Fig. 4.1.4)

> And they lived happily ever after!
>
> The end

page five (Fig. 4.1.5)

> But wait there's a moral to this story
> "You shoud always be happy for who you are"

The Lion and the Tiger

Fig. 4.1.1

Fig. 4.1.2

CHAPTER FOUR: TRANSITIONAL REVISION

Fig. 4.1.3

Fig. 4.1.4

The Lion and the Tiger

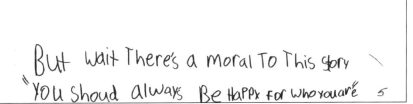

"But wait There's a moral To This story
"You shoud always Be HapPy for who you are   5 | *Fig. 4.1.5*

Clearly Amanda is capable of telling a different version of a story, knows fiction from nonfiction, literal from non-literal meanings. She writes in complete sentences, correctly punctuates the interrogative, comprehends the text features of a fable—with that wonderful "But wait there's a moral to this story." What voice Amanda has! Her story holds a beginning, middle, and an ending. The conflict is resolved and the theme explicit.

Amanda created her book, which she "published" and shared, in basic book format, complete with page numbers. Her moral demonstrates her ability to persuade, to convince others of her own thinking about what's important.

So what does Amanda need to ratiocinate? Looking at the teacher's objective, the curriculum, and the standards, but mostly analyzing Amanda's story, her teacher and I determined her story would have been helped had she used quotation marks around the dialogue. Her teacher said, "Amanda knows those marks. Look, she used them around the moral of the story, but she apparently does not know how to use them when someone is talking." Good appraisal. I concurred. Because Amanda's teacher expressed concern that most of her students were weak with quotation marks yet always use dialogue, we decided to use Amanda's story as a lesson for the entire class.

Chapter Four: Transitional Revision

Mentoring Lesson 3.
Quotation Marks and Commas with the Tag in Dialogue

I invited Amanda to sit in the "Author's Chair," share her story with class, which she did, and the kids loved it. Her teacher and I especially liked how she would read a page and then turn her book to show all the students her illustrations.

We made a copy of Amanda's book so she could mark it up but still retain the original. With all that in place, we asked Amanda to put page one on the document camera and "become the teacher."

Me: Amanda, you have a wonderful story here—you have written a fable. Do you know what makes a story a fable?

Amanda: It has animals and a moral.

Me: What exactly is a moral?

Amanda: A lesson. In case someone missed it, you put it at the end.

Me: Wonderful! Do you know what I like best in your fable?

Amanda: No.

Me: I like when you wrote on page 5—"But wait there's a moral to this story." I liked that you called your reader's attention to the moral.

Amanda: (smiling a big smile) I liked that, too.

Me: Why did you put those little marks, we call them quotation marks, around the moral, Amanda?

Mentoring Lesson Three

Amanda: Because I was telling the moral to the story.

Me: Oh, so you know that quotation marks go around what someone says?

Amanda: Yes, our teacher told us they are like little lips—they show when someone starts talking and when they stop talking.

Me: Well, let's look at some places on page two where someone talks and put red lipstick marks (crayon) around what that character says. Read page two again. When someone speaks, stop to put marks around what that character says.

Amanda: Reads up to "moning and groaning." Should I put them here (pointing to the words)?

Me: What a great question, Amanda. Let's figure out if those are the actual words lion says.

Amanda: (After some thinking) No, they aren't. I just tell that he is doing that.

Me: Good thinking, Amanda. Keep reading to see if either of your characters says something directly.

Amanda: She reads and stops excitedly. Here. Here is a place, pointing to *What is wrong?* Tiger asks lion that.

Me: Perfect. Put those little lips before the word *What* and after the question mark. (She does.) Now, Amanda, when we introduce what someone says with the word like *said* we put a comma after that word—like this (and I quickly show her *He*

CHAPTER FOUR: TRANSITIONAL REVISION

said, "What is wrong?") Let's put that comma in purple, Amanda, so we don't forget it. Purple to remember.

Amanda adds a purple comma and continues to *The lion said*. She immediately places a purple comma after *said* and quotation marks around *I'm sick. Oh, I wish I was not a lion!*

I nod approvingly as does Amanda's teacher. Amanda finishes the page in that manner.

We stop after page two and invite the class to check their stories for places where their characters speak. We remind them to put red lipstick quotation marks around their words. We caution them to remember to add the comma after the introductory word using their purple crayons.

Red quotation marks and purple commas did the trick; the colors and concepts quickly insinuated themselves into the minds of these transitional revisers. They had accepted the challenge rising to our expectations. As the teacher and I traveled around the room reading the students' papers, we found very few students who needed more nudging. We basked in their successes.

WHAT DID WE LEARN FROM AMANDA'S EXPERIENCE WITH RATIOCINATION?

- stories with animals as characters are called fables
- the moral of the story is a stated, explicit theme, message, or lesson
- direct words of characters go inside quotation marks
- words like *said* that introduce the direct words of characters are followed by a comma
- writing a story with beginning, middle, end
- reinforcing fables
- writing and publishing a book
- orally sharing that book
- following directions

Once again, while Amanda is a young writer, we find older writers who are moving from imitating other texts to an understanding of the grammatical and syntactical structures of the language. No matter what the age of the "Amandas" you teach, recognizing where they are in the sequence of ratiocinating will help catapult them more quickly into deeper revision, a more profound sense of grammar, and

the rigor of writing.

    Always one of my favorites to teach, third-graders, in flux as they move from writing the "lists" of real life to more imaginative stories, which they root in real life, are eager learners and eager writers. They embody all that is best in the transitional revisionist because the reader can almost see the awakening of cognitive clarity. Best of all, unless they have that exuberance quelled by worksheets and mindless assignments, they recognize and revel in their own creativity. Mariana was no exception. Writing the following sample (Fig. 4.2) in February, Mariana delighted the class with her story.

Ernie the Eraser

There was once an eraser maned Ernie. He was the only eraser in the classroom. The classroom was in a land called perfict. It was called that because no/one ever made mistakes. So no/one ever ever payed attention to Ernie.

One day a little girl was writing and made a mistake. She started crying. Ernie heard her. So he hopped out of the suplly dwawer and asked the girl why she was crying. She told him about making a mistake. So Ernie said "I'll fix that" so he erased It for her and Ernie became a hero. He was then never forgotten.

    THE END

Chapter Four: Transitional Revision

> Mariana
>
> ## Ernie the Eraser
>
> There was once an eraser named Ernie. He was the only eraser in the classroom. The classroom was in a land called perfist. It was called that because nopne ever made mistakes. So ndone ever ever payed attention to Ernie. One day a little girl was writing and made a mistake. She started crying. Ernie heard her. So he hopped out of

Fig. 4.2.1

Ernie the Eraser

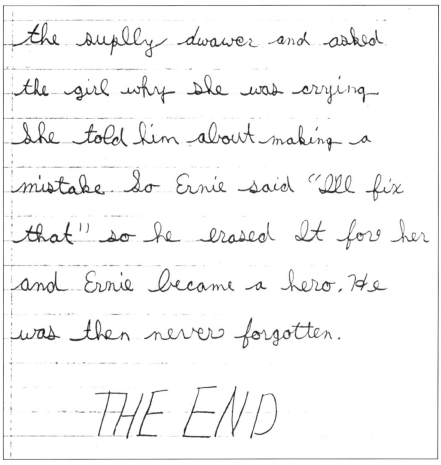

Fig. 4.2.2

In analyzing Mariana's writing, I found a coherent piece of discourse. Her sentences flow as sentence two connects to sentence one, three to two and so on. Each sentence progresses logically from what comes before to what follows. The controlling idea of "Ernie" is consistent; she has supporting sentences with details and explanation, and a conclusion. Her story, although grounded in the reality of a classroom, is imaginative.

While Mariana mixed her *m* and *n* in the word *named*, I saw that as a minor slip. *Perfict* comes close to the correct spelling, the second *l* in *suplly* instead of the second *p*, and the *w* instead of *r* in *dwawer* were not serious spelling blunders, all easily corrected, especially considering how she correctly spelled words such as *eraser, mistakes, attention, hopped, crying, hero*. *Payed* is simply

CHAPTER FOUR: TRANSITIONAL REVISION

an over application of adding the suffix *–ed* to the root. I didn't want to get into *payed vs paid* since *The American Heritage Dictionary*, while preferring *paid*, accepts both.

Further, her punctuation reflects a literate third-grade student: She only missed the comma after *said*, the one between *ever and ever,* and another after *that*. She correctly contracts *I will (I'll)* and uses quotation marks properly.

What should Mariana ratiocinate?

Although I wanted to work with Mariana on her paragraphing—indenting *One day*—I felt given Mariana's creativity and her love of writing, this paper marked a good time to call attention to the "to be" verbs. She has a preponderance of them.

MENTORING LESSON 4
"TO BE" VERBS

Me: Mariana, you have such a wonderful story here. Would you read it aloud to me?

Mariana: Oh, yes.

Me: Want to know what I like best in your story?

Mariana: Oh, yes.

Me: I like the way the story flows. It was easy to follow; that's important for readers so authors always try not to lose their readers. Did you like writing this story?

Mariana: It was funny. I was writing about mistakes and then I saw I put *no* and *one* together, so I just made a line between the two words.

Me: All writers make mistakes on their early drafts.

Mentoring Lesson Four

	What draft was this?
Mariana:	My first draft after prewriting. Our teacher had us do like a house print. Everybody picked their own rooms or their grandma's house, but I thought of a classroom. My teacher thought it was neat that I made an eraser a character.
Me:	Do you know what that's called, Mariana?
Mariana:	The teacher told me it's like making a person, so it's called persification or something like that.
Me:	Close enough—personification.

Mariana repeats the word.

Me:	Did you find any other things you could make better in your writing?
Mariana:	Probably some spelling words.
Me:	Why don't you just underline those and we can check on them later, OK?

Mariana underlines *suplly* and *dwawer*.

Me:	Good. Well, I think you are such a good writer I wonder if you'd like to do something published writers do.
Mariana:	I'd like that.
Me:	Remember when we played "Simon Says" and your teacher had you clap, turn around, touch your nose, and all those actions?

CHAPTER FOUR: TRANSITIONAL REVISION

Mariana: That was fun!

Me: Those were all action verbs. But remember when she said, "Simon Says 'was' and everybody just looked at her because they didn't know how to do 'was'?

Mariana: I remember. We just stood. We did that with some other words, too, like *is*.

Me: Do you remember what your teacher said?

Mariana: That there were action verbs and another kind.

Me: You have a good memory, Mariana. Those other verbs just show something exists—that's why everyone just stood.

Mariana: Cool.

Me: Well, you have several of those exist verbs in your writing. It might be fun to see if any of them could be turned into action verbs. Want to try?

Mariana: Oh, yes.

Me: Why don't you play detective and see if you can find the exist verbs. Think of them as clues in your writing. Take your highlighter and highlight *was* every time you see it in your paper. (I write the word *was* on the board.)

Mariana sets to work. At one point she looked at me and said, "I have a bunch of *wases*!"

Me: Let's count how many you have, Mariana.

Mentoring Lesson Four

      Mariana: Seven!

      Me: Let's read your first few sentences to see if you can think of an action verb to use instead of *was*.

At this point I show Mariana what I did in my paper.

Before:

Our Pied Piper was not like the one in the original story.

After:

Our Pied Piper did not resemble the one in the original story.

      Me: Here, Mariana, I just replaced *was not like* with *did not resemble*. You might try that. If you do that you have decoded your clue.

                  Another way to decode would be to change your sentences around or combine them to make a longer sentence. Let's see if I did that in my paper. (I model scanning my paper.) Sort of, and I did put two sentences together to get rid of an exist verb.

Before:

Our Pied Piper was dressed in baggy pants. He was foreign. He brought a monkey along with his music box.

After:

Our foreign-looking Pied Piper dressed in baggy pants and brought a monkey along with his music box.

87

CHAPTER FOUR: TRANSITIONAL REVISION

Me: You see here, Mariana, I moved *foreign* from the predicate part of the sentence to an adjective describing *Pied Piper*. I added *looking* because it sounded better than just *foreign*. When I did that I could drop the sentence *He was foreign*. Then I connected the last sentence to the first sentence with *and*. Do you see that?

Mariana: I didn't know you could do that.

Me: Sure you can. Now read your first couple of sentences and see what you can decode.

Mariana: "There was once an eraser maned Ernie." Eeek! it should be *named*.

Me: Good catch, Mariana. Let's go to the next sentence.

Mariana: "He was the only eraser in the classroom."

Me: Now can you think a way to decode those sentences to get rid of at least one *was*?

Mariana makes several attempts. She decides she can't change the first sentence, so she does what I did—she combines them.

Mariana: I think I could say, *There was once an eraser named Ernie.* I like that because it sounds like the beginning of a fairy tale—you know—like *Once upon a time*. So then could I just say *There was once an eraser named Ernie* and make one of those marks — *the only eraser in the classroom.*

Me: You sure could. You could also put a comma after

Mentoring Lesson Four

        Ernie and then write *the only eraser in the classroom.* The dash is bolder whereas the comma sort of gentles in the information. Which do you want? You are the author.

Mariana: Hmmmm. I want the dash.

Me: OK. Now I'm going to let you work some more on your decoding.

At the end of the reading/writing workshop period, Mariana showed me her paper.

    There was once an eraser named Ernie—the only eraser in the classroom. The classroom was in a land called perfict because no one ever made mistakes. So no one ever ever needed Ernie. One day a little girl made a mistake in her writing. She started crying. Ernie heard her. So he hopped out of the supply dwawer and asked the girl why she was crying. She told him about making a mistake. So Ernie said "I'll fix that" so he erased it for her and Ernie became a hero. He was then never forgotten.
    THE END

Mariana reduced her "to be verbs" from seven to four. Further, given permission to change things, she changed *payed attention to Ernie* to the much more accurate and concise *needed Ernie*. Quite a feat for a first-time effort.

Quickly I showed her the correct spelling of *supply* and *drawer*.

Mariana: Oh, I can change those faster than fast.

Me: That's the neat part about writing, Mariana, you can go back and correct those mistakes. You are a good little writer. Keep writing.

Chapter Four: Transitional Revision

What did we learn from Mariana's ratiocination?

- changing "to be" verbs to action verbs
- replacing words with synonyms
- rearranging sentences
- combining sentences
- turning choppy sentences into longer sentences—more mature syntax
- catching spelling errors
- how to code and decode (revise) writing
- making important decisions about writing
- the difference between a dash and a comma
- following a model helps understanding

Quite frankly, if "Ernie the Eraser" had been typed out with all correct spelling and punctuation, my guess is that many would think an adult had written the story for children. My point is that grade level has little to do with creativity but an encouraging environment has everything to do with creativity. What Mariana ratiocinated could easily be done in middle school or high school or even by kids in college. Those "to be" verbs are often the mark of lazy writers, who grab at the first verb that pops into their heads instead of ratiocinating—thinking—their way into the more precise verb.

Chapter Five
Medial Revision On-level Understanding of Grammatical and Syntactical Structures Stephen and Nellie

As we move into medial revision, I shall dispense with the dialogue I used to demonstrate how ratiocination works with younger students or with students newer to the act of authentic writing. Here I take a more analytic stance, using the following procedure:

- the original writing (the before)
- an analysis
- a prioritizing
- ratiocination strategy or strategies
- possible lesson topics—to show how ratiocination taps the richness of writing
- revised writing (the after)
- evaluation.

Be clear that while I offer many lesson suggestions, I don't expect teachers to attempt each one. These suggestions merely show the myriad possibilities—the many grammar lessons nestled within so simple a strategy as coding a clue and decoding it. But, as always, teachers determine the best lessons.

Chapter Five: Medial Revision

Because so many ELAR standards include expository essays and the writing process: prewriting, writing (drafting), revising, and editing, I chose Stephen's work. Stephen, who always did his work but was not the best student in the class, typifies an average medial student attempting to explain the ills of homework.

His prewriting sets up what follows in his hand-written draft, which he ratiocinated. He typed his final copy.

The original writing (before)

I would like not to have any homework on the weekdays and the weekends.

It would allow teachers not to think as much about assignments. You see they have to make up assignments on either Math, Science, Social Studies, or Language Arts (incase you didn't allready know that). They spend alot of time on just that it would make it easier if they didn't have to do that.

The grades might improve because of less work. Everyday when children get homework they get tired now give us a break people. We do homework just about everyday, everyday now we get tired.

Also the mothers and fathers wouldn't have to worry about when, and if the homework was done. Now our parents are always yelling at us about when our homework is finished, and I get tired of that. So please let the kids have a break from homework.

The kids at school would be "Happy," and could go outside to play right away. Having no homework would be the greatest thing that happened to kids (and let me tell you something the person who does away with homework would be a saint). So, in conclusion, I plead to give kids a break.

Analysis

AN ANALYSIS

PROS

Stephen obviously feels strongly about this issue of homework, so he clearly establishes his central idea in the first paragraph, but his paper, more persuasive than informative or explanatory, does not exactly fit expository writing. Using the basic structure of an essay—introduction, body, conclusion, Stephen moves from teachers to grades, to mothers and fathers, and finally to kids. This progression of people affected by homework, while appropriate, meanders to "grades" in paragraph two. Still, the paper is organized. His asides, which he correctly places in parentheses on two occasions, add voice.

CONS

Stephen's essay lacks depth in its development of ideas. List-like, he doesn't provide much explanation—this is deadly for an expository essay. Poor transitions hurt his coherence while the run-on sentences hurt his communication.

It seems Stephen is trying too hard for five paragraphs.

As it stands, though, Stephen's essay contains many opportunities to teach grammar within the writing process and provides even more opportunities for revision and editing.

Grammar/revision/editing Opportunities:

- compound words—Stephen compounds some words erroneously: *incase, allready, alot*
- he misuses *either* by using it before more than two subjects
- his external transitions—from paragraph to paragraph—are non existent except for one thereby weakening the essay's coherence of ideas
- his internal transitions—from sentence to sentence could be strengthened
- although his points are sound, the details supporting them are weak

93

Chapter Five: Medial Revision

- some of his sentences are wordy
- he has run-on sentences
- there are some comma blunders

Prioritizing

- Sentences
- Transitions

The ratiocination strategy for sentences

Underlining each sentence in alternate colors encourages students to study their sentences. The decoding gives them strategies to make their sentences better, clearer, more sophisticated, smoother, and easier for the reader to follow and comprehend.

Code	Clue	Decoding
underline	sentences in alternate colors	Look for variation in length • if short and choppy, try combining sentences • if long and stringy, be sure they are not run-on sentences or comma spliced sentences consider subordinating conjunctions, coordinating conjunctions, or conjunctive adverbs check for the subject (the doer) and the verb (what is being done) re-read each sentence to see if every word counts

Ratiocination Stategies

THE RATIOCINATION STRATEGY FOR TRANSITIONS

Transitions carry the logic of writing into depth. Transitions that show progression from sentence to sentence cement the relationships among ideas. Typically, neophyte writers make a statement and then another and then another with no sense of progression, or they make a statement and follow it with a thin detail to make a paragraph and then they do exactly the same thing for succeeding paragraphs. Their writing is broad but not deep; it's developmentally an extension of the lists they loved to write in the primary grades.

Code	Clue	Decoding
a small hook (sentence)	beside the beginning of each sentence	Does sentence one connect to sentence two in some way, sentence two to sentence three, and so forth? • by repeating a word or using a synonym • with a transitional word • with a transitional phrase • by parallel structure • following chronologically • with an extended metaphor • by using imagery to chain together succeeding sentences
a bigger hook (paragraph)	beside the beginning of each paragraph	Does paragraph one connect to paragraph two in some way, paragraph two to paragraph three, and so forth? Use phrases such as • "Thinking ahead…" • repeating or rephrasing key words or terms to remind the reader what's been said Use clauses such as • "I moved on to…" • "When you know…" Think about "If/so" statements to bridge ideas.

Chapter Five: Medial Revision

Placing a hook as a code beside each sentence reminds students to hook (connect) their sentences together and placing a hook beside each paragraph reminds them to hook their paragraphs together with transitions.

Possible Lessons

Stephen dutifully underlined each sentence—one in yellow, the next in brown, and so on. He also drew a small hook after each sentence and a larger one next to each paragraph except the first.

I would like not to have any homework on the weekdays and the weekends.

Underlining the opening sentence enabled the following lessons:

- A discussion of the rhetorical purpose of a one-sentence paragraph. Was one sentence effective? Is it sometimes okay to have a one-sentence paragraph? For what reasons? Does it work here? Does it adequately prepare the reader for an explanation of his central idea of homework?
- Does the organization best fit the purpose of the paper—to explain homework?
- The central idea as focus and sustaining that focus.
- Do all the words in that first sentence carry their own weight? Could that sentence be said in a better way?
- What about the word order in that sentence—its syntax? Do we usually say "I would like not to have…"? How could we say that in a better way?

Possible Lessons

<u>It would allow teachers not to think as much about assignments.</u>

This next sentence introduces the second paragraph and allows for the following lessons:

- *It* is a pronoun. What noun is it replacing? Where is that noun? Is that an effective transition? What is the author expecting the reader to hold in his or her head?
- Moving from one paragraph to the next is like taking the reader's mind by the hand. Is there a better way to do that than by using *It*?

<u>You see they have to make up assignments on either Math, Science, Social Studies, or Language Arts (incase you didn't allready know that).</u>

This sentence is replete with possible lessons:

- *You see* directly addresses the reader and should have a comma after it.
- Changing rhetorical stance.
- Addressing the audience as *you* instead of the using the royal *we* or first person *I*.
- The word *on* is not usually used in this context. What word could be used that is more precise?
- *Either* is a used when referring to two items. What word could replace *either* since there are four items mentioned?
- *Incase* should be two words
- *Allready* should have one *l*

Chapter Five: Medial Revision

They spend alot of time on just that it would make it easier if they didn't have to do that.

Consider what lessons this sentence offers:

- It has been a while since we read the word *teachers*, so should *they* be replaced with its noun?
- *Alot* is two words
- The subject *They* and the verb *spend*
- What does the first *that* refer to? the second *that*?
- Demonstrative pronouns
- The subject and predicate (verb) in sentences
- Run-on sentences
- Possible punctuation to avoid run-on sentences, e.g. terminal marks, semi-colon, coordinating conjunctions preceded by a comma
- Simple, compound, complex, compound/ complex sentences

The grades might improve because of less work.

Stephen uses *less* correctly because it refers to the general quantity of work, but this sentence begins the third paragraph so it needs a stronger transition.

- Transitions from paragraph to paragraph. Teaching the concept that paragraph two needs to connect to paragraph one in some way and paragraph three to two and so forth.
- Transitions as aids for the reader focus in two directions—backward and forward.
- Transitional words, phrases, clauses
- The word *might*, while expressing a theoretical possibility, dilutes the power of the argument.

Possible Lessons

<u>Everyday when children get homework they get tired now give us a break people.</u>

Possible lessons:

- A transition or connection between "grades might improve" from the previous paragraph and children getting tired.
- Supporting information on why or how children get tired
- Run-on sentences
- Direct address
- Parenthetical statements
- Punctuation

<u>We do homework just about everyday, everyday now we get tired.</u>

Possible lessons:

- Comma splice
- Sentences
- Supporting information
- Strong and weak repetition

Chapter Five: Medial Revision

<u>Also the mothers and fathers wouldn't have to worry about when, and if the homework was done.</u>

Moving to the next paragraph, we find more possible lessons:

- Commas
- Transitional phrases and clauses instead of just transitional words

<u>Now our parents are always yelling at us about when our homework is finished, and I get tired of that.</u>

Possible lessons:

- Diction/word choice, e.g. "yelling"
- Verb tense, e.g. "is finished"
- Multi-meaning words, e.g. "tired" as used previously and "tired" in this sense
- The deliberateness of following the progression of ideas from the central idea to the end of the essay

<u>So please let the kids have a break from homework.</u>

Possible lessons:

- Commas
- Consistency of word choice, e.g. "children/kids"

Possible Lessons

<u>The kids at school would be "Happy," and could go outside to play right away.</u>

Possible lessons:

- correct use of quotation marks
- commas
- upper-case letters
- precision of language, e.g. "right away"
- transitions

<u>Having no homework would be the greatest thing that happened to kids (and let me tell you something the person who does away with homework would be a saint).</u>

Possible lessons:

- commas
- direct address

<u>Kids need a break.</u>

Possible lessons:

- punctuation
- powerful concluding sentences

Chapter Five: Medial Revision

Revised writing (after)

    Homework is a drag on kids. It drags down our attitudes and it drags down grades. If we didn't have homework, we would have a better attitude and grades would improve. We might turn an F to an A- if our attitude is good towards our work. But if we have a bad attitude about school, we might burn out.

    Homework is a drag on teachers. They have to make up homework assignments. You see they have to make up assignments on Math, Science, Social Studies, or Language Arts (in case you didn't already know that). They spend a lot of time on just that. Life would be easier for them if they didn't have to do all that work so we didn't either.

    Homework drags down our physical bodies. We need exercise to grow. We also need exercise for cardiovascular reasons. If we are in our room doing homework, we won't be getting exercise. My dad says, "Healthy children are smart children."

    Healthy, smart, and happy students without homework could go outside to play right after school. Having no homework would be the greatest thing that happened to students (and let me tell you something — the person who does away with homework would be a saint). Think about it — kids need a break.

EVALUATION

The first thing we notice is that Stephen's opening sentence is less wordy and more direct in his final copy than in his original. He understands that a central idea should be clear and concise, so he definitely worked to hone his awkward wordy first draft. Further, in his attempt at depth, he added some details about attitude that were not in the original.

    Stephen uses parallelism by repeating the structure of the first sentence,

Evaluation

"Homework is a drag on kids" in the first sentence of the second paragraph, "Homework is a drag on teachers," which helps his transition.

He continues this parallelism with the smooth transition, "Homework drags down our physical bodies." This revision shows considerable improvement over "It would allow teachers…"

The transition to paragraph four is awesome and apparently happened after a teacher conference and peer grouping. By repeating "Healthy, smart, and smart" he markedly improved coherence. He also added when they would go outside, which ties that meaning with a nice bow and doesn't leave the audience hanging.

Stephen radically changed his concluding sentence from a persuasive one "So, in conclusion, I plead to give kids a break." to one to a contemplative one "Think about it—kids need a break." This change in rhetorical stance is both sophisticated and telling. Stephen has learned the difference between trying to convince the reader and informing the reader.

His paper goes from 212 words to 209 words yet there is more depth, with each word carrying its own weight. The correction of run-on sentences is the major improvement in Stephen's work.

Seeing all this improvement points to the value of ratiocination, of teaching grammar within the writing process where it takes, and of the powerful payoff for taking time to revise.

WHAT DID WE LEARN FROM STEPHEN'S RATIOCINATION?

- improved diction
- central idea as the driving force
- details that matter
- parallelism
- strong repetition
- transitions
- coherence
- conclusion
- tighter more powerful writing
- the benefits of revision

Chapter Five: Medial Revision

As we move ratiocination deeper, we move into more sophistication. Yet, although students have been writing in school for years, and although they may feel more secure in their written expression, they manage at this stage to find new ways to muddle their writing.

In the next sample chosen for this stage, one by Nellie, we find a concise and interesting narrative, one with a defined focus, reasons for the characters actions and consequences, but her verbs muddled her meaning.

The original writing (before)

A Fabulous Reality

The busy street and the noisy traffic were almost like home. If she would stop and close her eyes, trying to remember the familiar voices on the street, she would hear people talking, but it was not like home. The language was all so strange. It was almost frightening, yet when she opened her eyes, she could see smiling friendly faces and everything seems more promising.

Maria entered the department store to buy what she needed. All this was new to her because she was a Cuban refugee. It was very difficult for her to talk to the saleslady.

The saleslady offered her assistance. Maria was afraid to answer because she did not know how to speak English.

The saleslady realized Maria could not understand English. She tried to help Maria by picking up items, but Maria would say, "no" every time.

Finally, the saleslady showed Maria a pair of socks. The Cuban lady's showed approval, and she said, "*eso si que es!*"

The saleslady smiled and remarked, "Gosh! If you knew how to spell it, why didn't you tell me?"

(Note: *eso si que es* means, "Yes, that's it," in English but the English pronunciation is S O C K S!)

Analysis

An analysis

Pros

Nellie knows the elements of a narrative. She opens her story with setting and intrigue. Readers are introduced to the main character as "she," which disorients us, yet it works because momentarily we get caught up in the main character's disorientation. By the second paragraph we know "she" is Maria. The plot moves along quickly and coherently—this is a good piece of flash fiction.

Nellie has the sense of a storyteller and takes the risk of language play. Even if readers don't read Spanish, her explanation is clear and funny. Nellie's conclusion ties up her story with a satisfying bow.

Cons

Nellie's story lacks specificity. We long to know what city Maria associates with home, and we long to know what city was not home.

Most importantly, though, is Nellie's apparent confusion with tense. On the one hand, Nellie's use of *would* and *could* sounds irresolute, which grammatically adds to Maria's disorientation. On the other hand, her statements qualified with unnecessary conditionals—*would stop, would hear, was almost frightening* weaken the writing.

Some of her sentences could be combined and Nellie seems to either have a typo or a problem with the apostrophe.

Grammar/revision/editing Opportunities

- specificity
- verb choice (diction)
- verb tenses
- syntax
- the use of the apostrophe
- transitioning from the general to the specific

Chapter Five: Medial Revision

Prioritizing:

- verb choice
- verb tense

Ratiocinating Verbs

Knowing Nellie, the teacher decided to take care of the specificity problem through a mini-conference. He asked Nellie where Maria lived before and where she lived now. That simple question changed the face of the first paragraph. Nellie implemented the suggestion even before she began to ratiocinate.

Ratiocinating Verbs

Code	Clue	Decoding
highlight	all verbs and verb phrases	Check for the "to be" verbs and (since this had been ratiocinated before, students were familiar with the procedure)
		Check for the overuse of *could* and *would* • Does the *could/would* suggest doubt or uncertainty?
		Consider if the simple past, present, or future tense would make the writing more powerful, more direct, easier to follow?
		Does the *would* express a habitual or repeated action? Is it coupled with a phrase such as "once a week" or "every day"? If so, drop the *would* for tighter more emphatic writing.
		Make certain that the tense chosen is the tense meant. If everything is in the past tense, don't throw in a future tense or a present tense. Check for that as it confuses the reader.
		Sometimes a verb phrase points out a wordy sentence. Decode by considering the worth of every word in the sentence.

Chapter Five: Medial Revision

The Highlighted Version

A Fabulous Reality

The busy street and the noisy traffic were almost like home. If she would stop and close her eyes, trying to remember the familiar voices on the street, she would hear people talking, but it was not like home. The language was all so strange. It was almost frightening, yet when she opened her eyes, she could see smiling friendly faces and everything seems more promising.

Maria entered the department store to buy what she needed. All this was new to her because she was a Cuban refugee. It was very difficult for her to talk to the saleslady.

The saleslady offered her assistance. Maria was afraid to answer because she did not know how to speak English.

The saleslady realized Maria could not understand English. She tried to help Maria by picking up items, but Maria would say, "no" every time.

Finally, the saleslady showed Maria a pair of socks. The Cuban lady's showed approval, and she said, "*eso si que es!*"

The saleslady smiled and remarked, "Gosh! If you knew how to spell it, why didn't you tell me?"

(Note: *eso si que es* means, "Yes, that's it," in English but the English pronunciation is S O C K S!)

POSSIBLE LESSONS

Nellie highlighted all her verbs and verb phrases and was aghast at the number of "to be" verbs and empty phrases she found.

Nellie first decided on the time (tense) for her story. She re-read it and chose to write it in the simple past. "That's when it happened," she quipped.

Highlighting the verbs and verb phrases enable more lessons than those on verbs. Consider the following possibilities:

- the use of *would* and *could* as conditional words
- the use of *would* to express a habitual or repeated action.
- transitions from the general to the specific (as from the first paragraph to the second in this piece) "In narrative writing, always indicate the transition from the general to the particular—that is, from sentences that merely state a general habit to those that express the action of a specific day or period. Failure to indicate the change will cause confusion" (Strunk & White, 94).
- the tense time line (see *Brushing Up on Grammar,* Carroll and Wilson)
- choosing active verbs over "to be" verbs
- choosing the precise verb
- discussing the syntax as in "Maria was afraid to answer because she did not know how to speak English." What could make this sentence tighter, less wordy? Rework that sentence many ways to see possibilities.

Afraid to answer, Maria did not speak.

Maria, afraid to answer, did not speak English.

CHAPTER FIVE: MEDIAL REVISION

Maria did not speak English, so she was afraid to answer.

Maria who did not speak English did not answer.

Maria, afraid because she did not speak English, remained silent.

- the use of the apostrophe
    forming the possessive singular of nouns by adding 's
    forming the possessives of pronouns with no apostrophe
    review *its* and *it's*
- Show rather than tell for specificity in writing
- Use of imagery for specificity in writing
- The concrete versus the abstract when writing
- restrictive and non restrictive clauses

Evaluation

Revised writing (after)

The busy street and noisy traffic reminded her of Havana. If she stopped, closed her eyes, and tried to remember the familiar voices on the street, she heard people talking. But Houston was not Havana. The unfamiliar language sounded strange, almost frightening, yet when she opened her eyes, she saw smiling friendly faces and everything seemed more promising.

Maria entered the department store to buy what she needed. All this was new to her because she was a Cuban refugee.

A saleslady offered her assistance, but Maria had difficulty talking to her. She was afraid to answer because she did not know how to speak English.

The saleslady realized Maria did not understand her, so she tried to help by picking up items. Maria said, "no" every time.

Finally, the saleslady showed Maria a pair of socks. The Cuban girl approved, and said, "*eso si que es!*"

The saleslady smiled and remarked, "Gosh! if you knew how to spell it, why didn't you tell me?"

Note: *eso si que es* means, "Yes, that's it." in English but the English pronunciation is S O C K S!

EVALUATION

Being specific about Havana and Houston changed the complexion of the piece from the outset. Changing some of the "to be" verbs enlivened the piece and led to other changes. For example, "The busy street and the noisy traffic were almost like home" became tighter and more precise as "The busy street and the noisy traffic reminded her of Havana."

Changing the highlighted verbs to the simple past helped Nellie's writing

CHAPTER FIVE: MEDIAL REVISION

become more consistent, less confusing. She also caught the present tense of *seems* that made no sense in context; it needed to be in the past tense.

Nellie knows a thing or two about varying her sentence lengths with that corker "But Houston was not Havana," which she tucked neatly between two long, syntactically mature sentences. That single stylistic trick emphasized the two cities and Maria's disorientation.

"The language was all so strange" morphed beautifully into the phrase "The unfamiliar language…" the adjective *unfamiliar* aptly taking care of the "to be" verb and the rather empty phrase "was all so strange."

Highlighting illuminated the weak repetition of "showed" in the fifth paragraph. Nellie chose to change the second *showed* to *approved*, which created a better image. She also changed *lady's* to *girl*, explaining that sounded truer and she further explained that she meant *lady's approval* but discovered that didn't work either. "The Cuban lady's approval, and she said…" made no sense.

Nellie decided not to change anything on her ending.

WHAT DID WE LEARN FROM NELLIE'S RATIOCINATION?

- specificity
- active verb choices
- one change often leads to another
- varying sentence lengths
- stylistic choices
- strong versus weak repetition
- diction
- a conclusion with POP

Medial revision demands knowledge on-level; it insists upon rigor. Not that the kids are on-level when they enter this stage, but that they are on-level when they leave this stage. Their developing brains are able to handle more depth, and if scaffolded properly, especially when applied to their own writing, can manipulate the grammar and syntax with a degree of maturity. Ratiocination enables that scaffolding.

Chapter Six
Elevated Revision Genuine Conceptual Understanding, Reaching Grammatical and Syntactical Maturity in Style, Tone, Craft Alexandra

We arrive at elevated revision with ratiocination still a viable option for revising, for reviewing grammar, for in-depth work on craft, or for all those options. As we know, writing can always be improved. But improvement at this level calls upon an intense sense of audience and purpose, control over the central idea, facility with language as well as the security to take compositional risks.

Alexandra, a twelfth-grade student in AP Honors English contributed several drafts of a piece she entitled: I Remember "Mama." Thinking this an allusion to the old forties movie or the fifties TV show by the same name, I was drawn to her essay. Instead, I discovered well wrought writing about one word—*mama*. I immediately thought *Now, that's a compositional risk*.

Fully developed, this essay runs eleven paragraphs in length—too long to repeat multiple times here, so I will show the development of her first paragraph over multiple drafts and conclude with the entire piece.

Chapter Six: Elevated Revision

The original writing of the first paragraph

No title

While writing this paper ~~I have~~ about words I have thought of different ~~wg~~ ways in which I could make my paper interesting or unique. ~~I have though~~ A paper on the obscurity of meaning of words used in law might be interesting, or a paper on words that sound or look romantic, or words that ~~a~~ sound important ˰ may also be interesting. "Words that sound important" seems like a good place to start. Peace, war, education, transportation, initiation, postulation all sound ~~in~~ important. Well, okay, how about beautiful words: mercurial, wind, melody, harmony, jasper, silence. ~~all beautiful wor~~ I could go on and on with lists, but instead I have decided to choose ~~an~~ a word that is importantant in our language, a word that sounds really interesting but I choose this word not ~~ben~~ only because of the way it looks, or sounds, it definition but it's meaning to me.

An Analysis

Pros

Clearly Alexandra, exposed to writing as a process for years, finds prewriting a comfortable means of finding an idea. She almost dialogues with self as she explores "interesting or unique meanings of words." Through this prewriting she presents herself with words, considers them, and then dismisses them. She crosses out, expunges, adds (correctly using the caret), and even occasionally misspells in her eager pursuit of her focus.

Cons

Alexandra produced a random first paragraph. While it reads almost like stream of consciousness and might be construed as sloppy, for example *importantant*, or careless writing to those uninitiated to prewriting, it harbors some nuggets that ratiocination can help.

Her tone is too informal for a formal essay on words, for example, "Well, okay…." Vacillating among various words strikes the reader as lack of focus, as filling a page with vacant writing. Alexandra repeats words such as *sounds* and *words* and *I* too often.

Grammar/revision/editing Opportunities

- thesis statement/controlling idea
- tone
- voice
- its/it's
- spelling
- weak repetition

CHAPTER SIX: ELEVATED REVISION

PRIORITIZING

- thesis,/controlling idea/central idea
- repetition of I

RATIOCINATING FOR THE THESIS STATEMENT

Unlike the search for the concrete "to be" verb, listing first words in a sentence, or underlining sentences in alternate colors, ratiocination for controlling idea bumps the process up to a much more sophisticated level.

A direct teach on thesis statement would be in order here.

Direct Teach I
Thesis Statement

- Quickly point out to students the thesis statements in several newspaper and magazine articles.

- Give students several newspapers and magazines and ask them to find the controlling idea in at least three or five articles.

- Explain that when reading, we call the controlling idea the *main idea*, *controlling idea*, or *theme* whereas in writing, we call the controlling idea the *thesis statement* or *proposition*, *specific controlling idea*, or *central idea*. The terms are interchangeable but the concept is invaluable. Help students realize no matter its name, if the reader is not clear about the writer's intent, the paper loses all impact.

In Alexandra's case (and this strategy works with others having this problem), I asked Alexandra to box up each of the ideas she presented in her first paragraph, list them like a grocery list, and then star the one she thinks she could write about best.

116

Ratiocinating for the Thesis Statement

　　　While writing this paper ~~I have~~ about words I have thought of different ~~wg~~ ways in which I could make my paper interesting or unique. ~~I have though~~ A paper on the obscurity of meaning of words used in law might be interesting, or a paper on words that sound or look romantic, or words that ~~a~~ sound important may also be interesting ^ . "Words that sound important" seems like a good place to start. Peace, war, education, transportation, initiation, postulation all sound ~~in~~ important. Well, okay, how about beautiful words: mercurial, wind, melody, harmony, jasper, silence. ~~all beautiful wor~~ I could go on and on with lists, but instead I have decided to choose an a word that is importantant in our language, a word that sounds really interesting but I choose this word not ~~ben~~ only because of the way it looks, or sounds, it definition but it's meaning to me.

words

I have thought different
interesting or unique
obscurity of meaning of words in law
that sound or look romantic
sound important
peace

CHAPTER SIX: ELEVATED REVISION

war
education
transportation
initiation
postulation
beautiful words
mercurial
wind
melody
harmony
jasper
silence
** not only looks or sounds, it definition, but it's meaning for me

POSSIBLE LESSONS

- controlling idea as thesis statement
- introductory paragraphs
- text structures
- creating list of words that are important to her
- tone as a reflection of attitude
- tone as the result of allusion, diction, figurative language, imagery, irony, symbol, syntax, and style
- rhetorical stance
- its/it's
- checking spelling
- circling the *Is*
- repetition—strong and weak

Revised writing (after)

There were two intervening drafts between the prewriting and this final draft.

I Remember "Mama"

I have thought about different ways I could write an essay about one interesting or unique word. Many words look beautiful or make beautiful sounds for the ear, but a word's real importance lies in the feelings it evokes. I decided to choose a word to explore to its depth and zenith not only because of the way it looks or sounds, but also for its definition and complexity. That word is **mama**.

Mama comes naturally to the mouth and ear. The word is a combination of two sounds, "mmmm" and "ah."

When you say, "mmmm" you usually mean that something appeals to you—the taste of chocolate, the smell of flowers, an interesting thought or idea. Sometimes, though, "mmmm" means indecision or even frustration. This sound is easy to make. Put your lips together, like the start of a long lingering kiss, and let your voice hum "mmmm."

The other half of **mama** is a breath and a sound put together. "Ah" is like "mmmm" in that it can be the sound of reacting to something pleasant but "ah" can also be the sound of pain and sorrow.

When these sounds are put together, you get a sound that can be soft and beautiful or shrill and annoying, depending upon the speaker's tone or the repetition of the word. Usually the speaker gets a lovely sound out of the word, almost a whisper, close to the heartbeat.

To most people, **mama** means mother, but you can mean mother with other words. **Mommy, ma, mummy, mom, mother, mammy** and countless other spellings and variations can mean mother.

Chapter Six: Elevated Revision

The **mama** form lexically rises above the other versions. **Mommy** sounds rather wimpy and annoying. It has too many "m's," and that bothersome "y" at the end causes irritation. **Ma** sounds too much like the "baa" of sheep whereas **mummy** sounds like its trying too hard; it's snobbish. Besides, I get a picture of a mummy chasing a half-crazed woman in a B-grade movie when I hear that word. **Mom** is too abbreviated, and I think palindromic words are creepy. **Mother** is a word reserved for situations of anger, embarrassment, direct address, or explanation as in "Mother, do you have to wear those curlers in your hair?" or "This is my mother." **Mammy** sounds too much like Al Jolson crooning Swanee River. **Mama** is the perfect word—harmonious and rhythmical.

To most people, the word **mama** means mother, but to many **mama** means mother and father or mother or father. **Mama** is the equivalent of "parent" or "person who cares for me." **Mama** has nothing to do with anatomy. When I need my parents, and I am upstairs and they are downstairs, I usually yell "Mama!" I have no preference for either parent; I love them both the same, but **mama** just happens to be the more familiar word. Actually, my father usually answers me anyway.

When I think about the word **mama**, certain thoughts and sensations come to mind. I think about my parents when I was younger and when I would cling close to them. I can almost feel the warmth that radiated from them, and I can smell the musky sweetness of my father's cologne and the dreaminess of my mother's perfume. I can feel my father's hands braiding my hair into lopsided pigtails and my mother's hands straightening them out. **Mama** also brings feelings of frustration, sadness, and anger. I think about the awful things I've said to them and then the sweet pain of reconciliation with hugs and kisses and the life lessons they have given me. The word **mama** captures all those feelings and memories.

Mama holds security and love, beautiful memories, a sense of belonging, and home. A sacred word with meaning but no definition, **mama** is father just as it is mother. It is strength and vulnerability, a stepping stone to success and a connection to two people I love.

A word is just a group of letters, but personal associations with a particular word and what it conjures up makes it important. Just think how awful life would be if we had no way to express our feelings, to trigger thoughts, to have a way to hold things dear to us. There is power in words that hold so many treasures. And I am rich indeed.

EVALUATION

Alexandra's prewriting paid off in a tight, well-constructed opening paragraph. I dare say that she spent the most time crafting that paragraph—and it shows.

Gone are the repetitive *Is*. Gone is the indecisiveness. Instead we have a specific word that emerges as the controlling idea and it controls the remainder of her essay.

Alexandra manages to couple information on the word *mama* with the powerful Nestorian-type organizational pattern that allowed her to save her personal reflection on the word *mama* for her final justification.

In closing, Alexandra iterates the power of words and chooses a contemplative conclusion. She invites readers to consider how bereft life would be without a means to express themselves. She knows "readers love to mull over and ruminate upon something"; she knows "this cognitive chewing is best at composition's end" (Carroll, 121). Then she hits the reader with that syntactical exclamation point—her last sentence.

CHAPTER SIX: THE ROOTS OR RATIOCINATION

WHAT WE LEARNED FROM ALEXANDRA'S RATIOCINATION?

- the value of prewriting
- crafting a piece
- Nestorian organization
- a contemplative conclusion
- sentence lengths
- improved syntax

I Rest My Case

There can be no doubt when looking hierarchically at the writing from Emergent Revision to Elevated Revision that ratiocination not only encourages the rigor but also insists upon it. Writers move in tandem to expectations; they thrive on models; they grow through mentors—both people and texts—but most of all their brains love the challenge. When we deny students such strategy-based instruction we doom them to mediocrity. As Doug Lemov says in his wonderful book *Teach Like a Champion*,

> One of the problems with teaching is that there's a temptation to evaluate what we do in the classroom based on how clever it is, how it aligns with a larger philosophy, or even how gratifying it is to use, not necessarily how effective it is in driving student achievement. The techniques described here may not be glamorous, but they work. As a result, they yield an outcome that more than compensates for their occasionally humble appearance (6).

Ratiocination as a strategy may not be razzmatazz, but if implemented by knowledgeable teachers with great consistency within the context of students' writing, the results are indeed razzmatazz.

Ratiocination References

Bruner, Jerome S. *The Process of Education*. NY: Vintage, 1960.

_____. *On Knowing: Essays for the Left Hand*. NY: Atheneum, 1971.

Byatt, A. S. *The Children's Book*. NY: Alfred A. Knopf, 2009.

Caine, Renate Nummela & Geoffrey Caine. *Making Connections: Teaching and the Human Brain*. Alexandria, VA, 1991.

Carroll, Joyce Armstrong. *Dr. JAC's Conclusions: The Unicorns of Composition*. Spring, TX: Absey & Co., 2004.

_____. *Authentic Strategies*. Spring, TX: Absey & Co., 2007.

_____. *Brushing Up on Grammar*. CA: Libraries Unlimited, 2010.

Carroll, Joyce Armstrong & Edward E. Wilson. *Acts of Teaching* (2nd ed.). CT: Teacher Ideas Press, 2008.

Clark, Stephen W. *A Practical Grammar*. NY: A.S. Barnes & Co., 1853.

Collins, Carmen. *Read, Reflect, Write*. NJ: Prentice-Hall, 1984.

Cooper, Charles R. & Lee Odell (eds.) *Research on Composing*. IL: NCTE, 1978.

Dewey, John. *Democracy and Education*. (reprint) KY: Feather Trail Press, 2009.

_____. *The Quest for Certainty*. NY: Capricorn Books, 1960.

Edwards, Betty. *Drawing on the Right Side of the Brain*. NY: J.P. Tarcher, 1979.

Emig, Janet. *The Web of Meaning*. NJ: Boynton/Cook, 1983.

Florey, Kitty Burns. *Sister Bernadette's Barking Dog: The Quirky History and Lost Art of Diagramming Sentences*. NJ: Melville House, 2006.

Graham, Steve & Michael Hebert. *Writing to Read: Evidence for How Writing Can Improve Reading.* Washington, D.C. Alliance for Excellent Education, 2010.

Hart, Leslie A. *How the Brain Works*. NY: Basic Books, 1975.

References

LeDoux, Joseph. *Synaptic Self*. NY: Penguin, 2002.

Lemov, Doug. *Teach Like a Champion*. CA: Jossey-Bass, 2010.

Noguchi, Rei R. *Grammar and the Teaching of Writing*. IL: NCTE, 1991.

Ornstein, Robert & Richard F. Thompson. *The Amazing Brain*. MA: Houghton Mifflin, 1984.

Poe, Edgar Allan. *The Dupin Mysteries and Other Tales of Ratiocination*. PA: Coachwhip Publications, 2009.

Ramachandran, V.S. *A Brief Tour of Human Consciousness*. NY: Pi Press, 2004.

Ratey, John J. *A User's Guide to the Brain*. NY: Pantheon Books, 2001.

Reed, Alonzo & Brainerd Kellogg. *Higher Lessons in English*. (reprint) KY: Hard Press, 2010.

Restak, Richard. *The New Brain*. NY: Rodale, 2003.

Smith, Frank. *Reading without Nonsense* (4th ed). NY: Teachers College Press, 2006.

Strong, William. *Sentence Combining* (2nd ed). NY: Random House, 1983.

Stull, William L. *Combining and Creating*. NY: Holt, Rinehart & Winston, 1983.

Vygotsky, Lev Semenovich. *Thought and Language*. Eugenia Hanfmann and Gertrude Vakar, editors and translators). MA: The M.I.T. Press, 1962.

_____. *Mind in Society*. (Michael Cole et al eds.). MA: The M.I.T. Press, 1978.

Weaver, Constance (ed.) *Teaching Grammar in Context*. NH: Boyton/Cook, 1996.

Wink, Joan & LeAnn Putney. *A Vision of Vygotsky*. MA: Allyn & Bacon, 2002.

Winterowd, W. Ross. *Contemporary Rhetoric*. NY: Harcourt Brace Jovanovich, 1975.

Young, Richard E., Alton L. Becker & Kenneth L. Pike. *Rhetoric: Discovery and Change*. NY: Harcourt, Brace & World, 1970.

Section Three
Thoughtful Practitioners

One of the champions of ratiocination in her classroom is fourth-grade teacher Emily E. Smith. Trained by trainers but exposed to ratiocination through her Abydos trainer mother, Smith has been using this method since she began teaching. As is the case with all good teachers, Smith observes her charges closely and listens to them even more closely. In this chapter she explains how that observation and listening resulted in not only better and deeper ratiocination in her students' writing but also an exciting way to apply ratiocination to literary analysis. Smith calls her adaptation "revertiocination."

—dr jac

Chapter Seven
Reverse + Ratiocination = Revertiocination: Literary Analysis

Emily E. Smith

As often as I read, I am reminded that the richness of a book isn't only found in the sum of its story, but equally from its individual words. Each word is as carefully arranged as a brick in the hands of a mason. I envy these published authors and—as the saying goes—I attempt to imitate them as my form of flattery. There arrives the wondrous challenge of burgling a complete stranger's mind. I had always planned on finding and harnessing this power of mimicry for myself, but it was my fourth grade class who made this most essential discovery.

While reading a passage from *Harry Potter and the Sorcerer's Stone* to my students, I stopped for a moment to point out how Rowling guided the reader into a comfortable flow with the use of varying sentence lengths. From the back of the carpet I heard an excited outburst, "Ratiocination! It's backwards! Backwards Ratiocination! Reverse Ratiocination!" Although it wasn't uncharacteristic for this particular student to gift me with little nuggets of knowledge, I was awestruck. How did I not think of this? I scrapped all of my current lessons and started from scratch. This new vision of revolutionizing the way we looked at accomplished authors' works became my number one priority. That night I stayed up well past my usual 9:30 curfew, hand-picking the most handsome passages from my favorite children's books. I scoured each text, analyzing sentence lengths, first words, and "to be" verbs. As I broke apart the strongest passages to uncover the secrets behind the authors, the phenomenon I sought lay right in front of me,

CHAPTER SEVEN: REVERTIOCINATION

answering questions like, 'Why does this paragraph sound so comfortable?' or 'How are simple words arranged to create an image that literally moves me?'

The Part Where We Discover

The next day I approached my class with the idea of reverse ratiocination. No denying that I was nervous. After all, the ratiocination strategy had become sacred within the walls of my classroom, and I didn't want to forsake—or disappoint—the name of something so precious. I began with a passage from the book that had catapulted forward the entire process, *Harry Potter and the Sorcerer's Stone*.

> Harry sniffed and a foul stench reached his nostrils, a mixture of old socks and the kind of public toilet no one seems to clean.
> And then they heard it—a low grunting, and the shuffling footfalls of gigantic feet. Ron pointed at the end of the passage to the left, something huge was moving toward them. They shrank into the shadows and watched as it emerged into a patch of moonlight.
> It was a horrible sight. Twelve feet tall, its skin was a dull, granite gray, its great lumpy body like a boulder with its small bald head perched on top like a coconut. It had short legs thick as tree trunks with flat, horny feet. The smell coming from it was incredible. It was holding a huge wooden club, which dragged along the floor because its arms were so long.
> The troll stopped next to a doorway and peered inside. It waggled its long ears, making up its tiny mind, then slouched slowly into the room.
> *Harry Potter and the Sorcerer's Stone*, J.K. Rowling, 174

As a class, we first tackled Rowling's use of sentence lengths. She followed no particular pattern, but certainly utilized a mixture of lengths. We classified them as long, medium, or short. For this passage, the variation went as follows: long, medium, long, medium, short, long, medium, short, long, medium, long.

We then discussed the purpose of using a variety of sentence lengths. How it felt comfortable to read in our heads. That it sounded natural when we read it out loud. By that time, the kids were clawing at the chance to dive into their own writing to see if they could create the "pattern of Rowling." They challenged themselves to see who could come closest to mimicking her style. This new concept turned my room into a mad literary hive—and not merely a fleeting excitement. It was as if we had unearthed this secret that was going to change the art of writing altogether.

The Part That Supports the Research

Reverse ratiocination was founded as a spin off—an ode to ratiocination and literary analysis alike. It remains a concrete, process-oriented strategy that uses students' texts as well as the works of published authors. Lev Vygotsky's research connecting cognitive development and language is also a component. His studies focused not only on the relationship of thought and words, but also the fundamental element of interaction.

Both ratiocination and reverse ratiocination are built around a core of engaged learners who become creators instead of bystanders. This strategy transforms students from temporary contributors into permanent problem solvers. Vygotsky's studies proved that language isn't merely a platform to tell, but rather an umbrella of understanding and meaning. Words are meant to be pushed and pulled and manipulated into something greater—springing from the uniqueness of our creativity and thought. Ratiocination is a tool that helps students journey toward an understanding of how precious imagination is when inventing language.

My first encounter with ratiocination was at the Capitol City Writes three-week training hosted by Abydos Learning (formerly New Jersey Writing Project in Texas). Reading along in *Acts of Teaching*, an immediate sigh of relief took over as I read, in depth, how I could integrate a unique, differentiated, and interactive revision strategy for tomorrow's thinkers.

The results were instantaneous—in *my* own writing. Never had I imagined how conceited it must seem that I started sentences with the word "I" twenty times

CHAPTER SEVEN: REVERTIOCINATION

within the period of 1,000 words. What was most unbelievable was how other teachers were receiving similar wakeup calls. Each realization fitting to his or her personal needs. I kept thinking that if something this straightforward could change the way I write, how could it change my students' writing?

The Part Where It Thrives in the Classroom

At that time, my teaching experience had consisted of two semesters of interning. In one month I was going to be thrown into a fourth-grade classroom with a testy air conditioner and a herd (yes, herd) of not-so-friendly cockroaches in South Austin. My heart and head burst with ideas and fears. After beginning the never-ending spiral of the writing process, the time came to introduce ratiocination. Over the course of a couple of days, I worked alongside my students (using some ideas from my three-week training) to conjure up exciting ways to revise. We imagined ourselves as detectives trying to crack the mystery of revision using all of our "secretive" codes.

The Part Where It Thrives in the Classroom

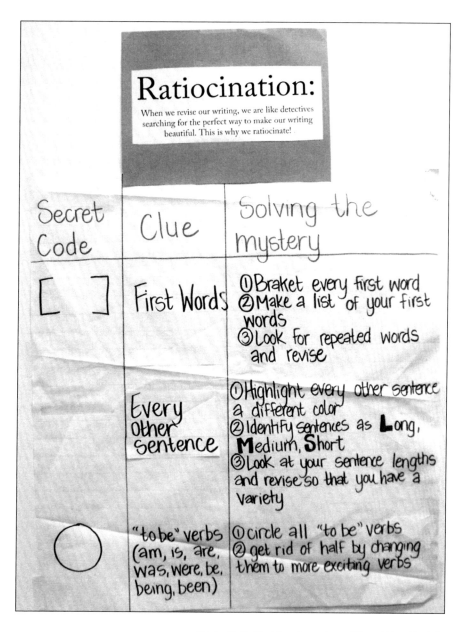

Fig. 7.1 Ratiocination: The Big Guide

This proved to be a great tool in the classroom, and it was one of our most beloved guide charts throughout the year. (Fig. 7.1)

CHAPTER SEVEN: REVERTIOCINATION

The Part Where It Gains Self-Awareness

The learning and growing never really ends on either side of the desk, now does it? Two years after my memorable first year, I stood with my jaw open in awe of the idea of reverse ratiocination, birthed from the mouth of a fourth grader. Taking a closer look at the strategy, I wanted to ensure that all of Vygotsky's underlying theories and research, as well as Carroll's practice of ratiocination, were upheld to the highest respect.

Wink and Putney put it most succinctly saying, "Vygotsky viewed the use of signs and symbols as mediators of human cognition. In other words, we use language…as a tool for developing thought." (*Vision of Vygotsky*, 47) Bells rang clear when I realized how ratiocination, or the use of signs and symbols, weren't just a convenient "code" that kids used in my classroom, they presented a gateway to higher development and literary analysis. My students were using all of the schema that they possessed on ratiocination and took it to the next level. To reverse ratiocination. I kept on thinking, "Dr. Carroll's gonna be so, so proud."

When I teach reverse ratiocination, I start with mentor texts to which the students can relate. I've found a passage by Roald Dahl, in his beloved creation, *Matilda*, to be quite the crowd pleaser. This particular excerpt is great to use when first starting out because it doesn't repeat any first words, contains very few "to be" verbs and uses only six sentences that vary in length. It makes the succinct point that writing is a delicate art form meant to be cherished and nurtured.

> Miss Trunchbull, the Headmistress, was something else altogether. She was a gigantic holy terror, a fierce tyrannical monster who frightened the life out of the pupils and teachers alike. There was an aura of menace about her even at a distance, and when she came up close you could almost feel the dangerous heat radiating from her as from a red-hot rod of metal. When she marched—Miss Trunchbull never walked, she always marched like a storm-trooper with long strides and arms aswinging—when she marched along a corridor you could actually hear her snorting as she went, and if a group of

The Part Where It Gains Self-Awareness

children were in her path, she ploughed right on through them like a tank, with small people bouncing off her to left and right. Thank goodness we don't meet many people like her in this world, although they do exist and all of us are likely to come across at least one of them in a lifetime. If you ever do, you should behave as you would if you met an enraged rhinoceros out in the bush—climb up the nearest tree and stay there until it has gone away.

Matilda, Roald Dahl p. 67

The first thing I have students do is act as if they are revising the piece using the strategy of ratiocination. They bracket first words, highlight every other sentence in a different color, and circle each "to be" verb. Witnessing that many students became overwhelmed with too much new information, I first have them just list the first words. This is the easiest way to engage them in the new process because it's immediately clear how carefully Dahl crafted his own first words.

This is a sample of my student, Marisa's, paper. (Fig. 7.2) Marisa even took the opportunity to point out how Dahl used an enormous amount of details to show and not tell. I believe that this wouldn't have been as evident to this student if she had not been reverse ratiocinating the piece in such an analytical manner.

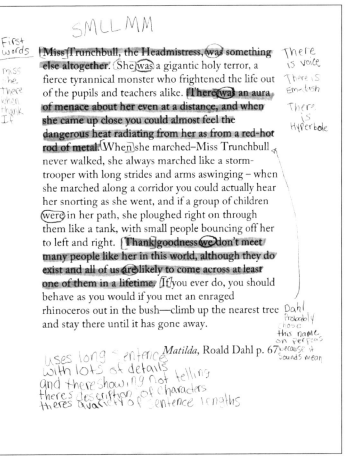

Fig. 7.2 Marisa's paper

CHAPTER SEVEN: REVERTIOCINATION

What Marisa did is evidence of Carroll's work, by means of equipping a student with the knowledge and skills to develop an understanding for herself rather than the teacher doing the interpreting. It sets the groundwork for stronger thinkers and creative writers. The scaffolding process moved from modeling to collaboration, then to an independent thought process.

The Part Where We Go Beyond

I began to observe more voice and confidence in my students' pieces and was amazed to find that, through literary analysis, many were imitating techniques in the passages we previously reverse ratiocinated. A passage from *Because of Winn-Dixie* proved to be an extraordinary jumping board for one of my students.

> My name is India Opal Buloni, and last summer my daddy, the preacher, sent me to the store for a box of macaroni-and-cheese, some white rice, and two tomatoes and I came back with a dog. This is what happened: I walked into the produce section of Winn-Dixie grocery store to pick out my two tomatoes and I almost bumped right into the store manager. He was standing there all red-faced, screaming and waving his arms around.
>
> "Who let a dog in here?" he kept shouting. "Who let a dirty dog in here?"
>
> At first, I didn't see a dog. There were just a lot of vegetables and green peppers. And there was what seemed like a whole army of Winn-Dixie employees running around waving their arms just the same way the store manager was waving his.
>
> And then the dog came running around the corner. He was a big dog. And ugly. And he looked like he was having a real good time. His tongue was hanging out and he was wagging his tail. He skidded to a stop and smiled right at me. I had never before in my life seen a dog smile, but that is what he did. Then he wagged his tail so hard that the knocked some oranges off a display, and they went rolling everywhere, mixing in with the tomatoes and onions and green peppers.
>
> *Because of Winn-Dixie,* Kate DiCamillo 1

The Part Where We Go Beyond

Aliza reverse ratiocinated this particular piece and was inspired to make some drastic changes. (Figure 7.3) in her own piece. She loved the way DiCamillo began her story with a long sentence that painted a vivid picture but was also moved by her use of short, succinct sentences to create drama. She was writing about an emotional move to Austin.

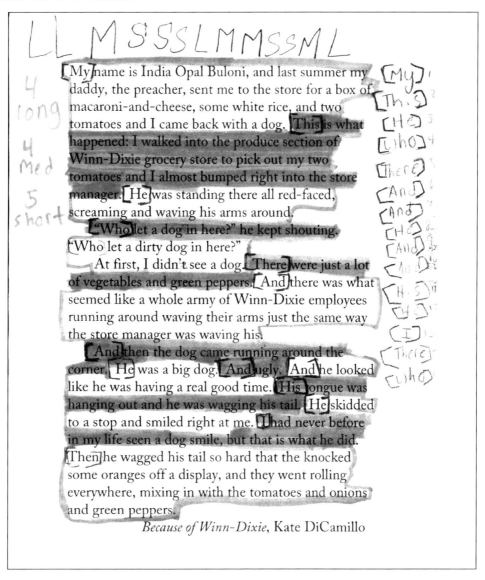

Fig 7.3—Aliza's coding

CHAPTER SEVEN: REVERTIOCINATION

Here is her lead: (Fig. 7.4)

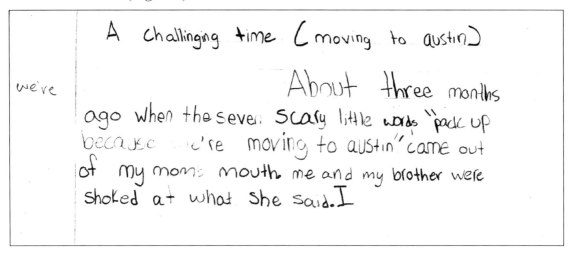

Fig. 7.4 Aliza's lead

Further into her text, she drew her readers in by implying that there was something wrong and that the move was necessary.

The Part Where We Go Beyond

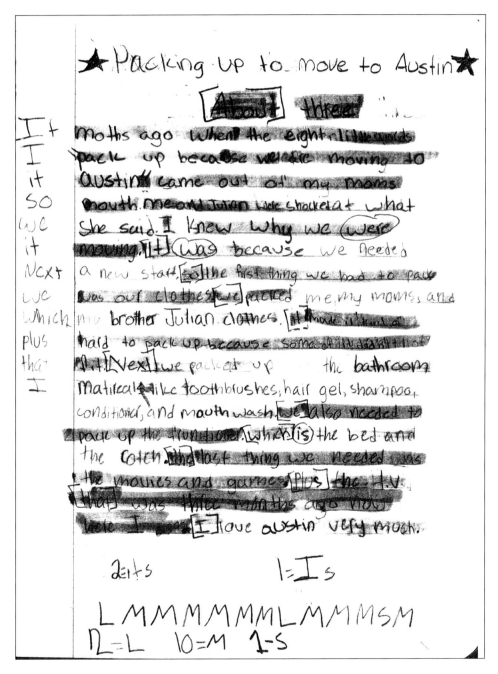

Fig. 7.5 Aliza's revision

CHAPTER SEVEN: REVERTIOCINATION

Here are some other student examples (before and after) that began to sprout up during our reverse ratiocination of the Winn-Dixie passage. First, we have Kellie's:

Before:

> Taylor held the bat straight and high. She was scared.

After:

> Though she was scared of getting hit by the ball, Taylor held the bat straight, high, and prideful.

Kellie noted that she enjoyed DiCamillo's use of winding sentences. I applauded the student because she had created, in her second drafting of this sentence, a rather enchanting movement.

Before:

> The weather was warm with some wind that wasn't cold.

After:

> The weather was a bit misty with a warm feeling and a good wind that wasn't cold.

Tia liked the way DiCamillo was detailed when talking about the oranges falling off the display. She wanted to do the same thing when she described the weather because she wanted her audience to feel what was happening.

Before:

> The cable car stopped and I was in Chinatown. It felt like a whole new world.

The Part Where We Go Beyond

After:

> I looked around and I said to myself, "what if I get lost?" With my eyes closed I walked forward. The sidewalk began. I opened my eyes and I was walking through the city. It felt like a whole new world.

My student, Emily, mimicked DiCamillo's purposefully choppy description of the dog. She liked that it sounded like how your brain would be working when it saw something for the first time.

Before:

> Ms. Jacob had her nose buried in the pages of a mysterious new book. Mr. Jacob noticed the letters of the book and it read "book death." Mr. Jacob got a bad feeling about that book.

After:

> Mr. Jacob's wife had her nose buried in the pages of a mysterious new book. Mr. Jacob noticed the letters of the book. It read "book death." He got a bad feeling about that book.

Alessandro noticed that DiCamillo used shorter sentences when the "danger" was coming (like when Winn-Dixie was running around the grocery store) and wanted to imitate this urgency in his writing. He wanted his readers to sense the "danger" coming not only in his words but also in his chosen sentence lengths.

Before:

> "Strike 1," said the umpire. "Strike 2."
> Cling. The ball was high. It was going really fast and it was going into the outfield.

Chapter Seven: Revertiocination

After:

> "Strike 1," said the umpire. Natalie focused on the ball. Her knees were bent and she was holding the bat. She stared at the ball. Cling. The ball was high and charging through the air into the outfield.

Kellie wanted to emulate DiCamillo's precise use of details. She shared with me that she was worried there were too few details in her first draft for the reader to be engaged. The student specifically mentioned when DiCamillo wrote that Winn-Dixie "skidded to a stop" rather than just stopping. Her addition of the ball "charging through the air" was inspired by this use of details.

The Part Where We Deem It Holy

Reverse Ratiocination quickly became a staple in the classroom, which meant that it deserved a highly coveted spot on our walls of guide charts. I wanted it to be accessible and personal, so we even decided to put up our humble suggestions for J.K. Rowling. Throughout the year we displayed many other passages that we reverse ratiocinated and students often visited them for inspiration. (Fig. 7.6)

The Part Where We Deem It Holy

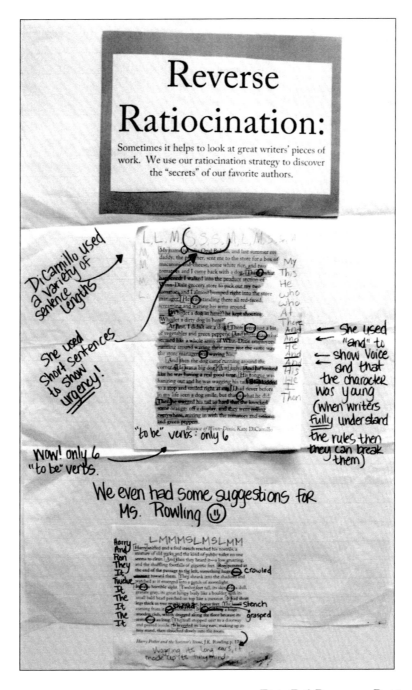

Fig. 7.6 Reverse Ratiocination

Chapter Seven: Revertiocination

As budding authors, many students would comment on how authors did repeat first words and even (gasp) used *and* at the beginning of the sentence. This was precisely what I wanted my students to notice as we investigated texts. I always tell them that once you fully understand the rules of writing, you then get to responsibly throw them out the window. They develop a love not only toward the mastery of language but also a true relationship with it, and they forever after seek those moments where the moment is perfect to color outside the lines.

The Part Where We Warm Up

I also incorporated warm-ups using reverse ratiocination. They were quick, enjoyable, and meaningful. As a class, we would work together to see if we could come up with an interesting story about something that had happened to all of us (e.g. field trip, reading outside, rainstorms, and so forth.) I challenged my students by making up a random pattern for sentence lengths and we had to, as a class, construct sentences that matched the pattern. We collaborated and rode piggyback off of each other to build a great little passage of writing.

The day after our school-wide field day, the class bubbled about our tug o' war win in the rain, so I thought, "Let's channel this energy into something purposeful." I gave them this sentence pattern challenge: Medium, short, long, short, medium (coded as MSLSM.) This is what we came up with:

> Everyone was excited because it was field day. Our hearts were pumping. The mist drizzled from the sky, enveloping our moving bodies, soaking our clothes and striking our skin. It didn't matter. We were determined to work as a team to pull our way to a muddy victory.

Here is another example of a warm up we completed as a class. I gave them the pattern: Long, long, medium, short, short, medium, long, short (coded as LLMSSMLS).

The Part Where We Warm Up

> The rain poured down while we slept, filling our courtyard garden like a swimming pool. When we walked into our classroom our precious books were scattered on the tables as Ms. Smith frantically tried to save them. Our hearts were just as torn as our books. What could we do? We felt destroyed. While the books were merely part of our classroom, they were still part of our hearts. Ms. Smith promised us that she would tell people our story and boy did people respond because we almost got ALL of our books back and safe in our arms. Our hearts danced with joy.

For students that needed an extra push, I would give the child his or her own sentence pattern challenge. One particular student, Zachius, was an amazing writer, but needed some definitive task to spark his creativity. Here is the sentence pattern I gave him: Medium, short, short, medium, short, long (coded as MSSMSL). He produced this:

> My team and I were warming up for our game. We were ready. And I was a little nervous. On our first play we did a wide receiver screen. I almost scored. I ran right past the other team, breaking tackles and jumping over people right and left.

The Part Where I Learn Something. Again.

These definitive warm-ups proved to be beneficial because they reinforce the research showing that specific and concrete strategies are necessary when teaching writing. Sometimes a minilesson that I viewed as a quick warm-up would

CHAPTER SEVEN: REVERTIOCINATION

turn into a weeklong exploration.

In one case, my initial goal in introducing this next piece was for my students to quickly look at sentence lengths and notice the healthy repetition of "if" as a first word.

> When I was a small boy, my grandmother told me about a distant uncle who was living in China during the Cultural Revolution. He promised to send a picture of himself to his relatives in America. If conditions were good, he said he would be standing. If they were bad, he would be sitting. In the photo he sent us, my grandmother whispered, he was lying down.
>
> As a Chinese American born in Southern California, my perception of China's Cultural Revolution was limited to stories that filtered out from the few relatives who stayed behind. As I grew older and China opened up to the West, I learned more.
>
> *Red Scarf Girl*, Ji Li Jang, XV

Students worked in partners to highlight every other sentence and to bracket each first word in each sentence. It was business as usual. Reverse ratiocination business, that is.

In our discussion about Jang's passage, one brilliant student, Alessandro, shared his thinking. Through the process of coding and then analyzing the first words, he noticed that the narrator switched tenses from the first paragraph to the second paragraph. He said that the narrator went from the past to the present. I wanted to know more about that so I asked him to explain his thinking. The student continued his reasoning by articulating that the author gave a little background information about the character before jumping into the story.

Wow. It's just like "time traveling," I thought aloud. We had to take advantage of this brilliant students' thinking. This was yet another golden idea birthed from the wonders of reverse ratiocination. I began to ask students if they had a background story that could lead up to their current pieces. We used large note cards to write a sentence or paragraph giving our readers a glimpse into the story behind our stories. Some students used these in their final drafts, some chose to stick with their current leads, and others even used them to inspire future pieces of writing. Here are some examples of my students' "time traveling" leads:

The Part Where I Learn Something. Again.

Every Christmas my family wakes up and goes downstairs. My brother and I see our stockings full and our presents around the tree. It's a beautiful sight to see.

I was born when some kind of white stuff fell on the third day of spring.

When we first met in third grade she was kind of shy. Well, I was too.

There has always been a huge tree close to my trampoline, but until that afternoon I had never thought about climbing it. That was the day I learned to fly.

Vygotsky calls this verbal thought—actively using our thoughts to produce language. We, as thinkers, often "time travel" in our thoughts, yet we don't physically produce language regarding our past memories. Sometimes these past memories play a valuable role in connecting our readers to the story we are trying to tell. Accomplished authors know the importance of the story before the story. These "time travelings" are the backbone and the support to many moments we write about. They are significant in our heads, but why aren't they significant in our writing? When students view and imitate passages that "time travel," they verbally think in a bigger context that is more vast and applicable to the story as a whole.

CHAPTER SEVEN: REVERTIOCINATION

The Part Where We Shift—like this...

Further into the year, I like to introduce more complex passages that begin playing with creative ways to use sequential listing and tone shifts. One of my favorite passages comes from the childhood classic, *Charlotte's Web*. What I love about this passage is that, through reverse ratiocination, students see an array of great sentence lengths that expose the thinking behind the text.

> The barn was very large. It was very old. It smelled of hay and it smelled of manure. It smelled of the perspiration of tired horses and the wonderful sweet breath of patient cows. It often had a sort of peaceful smell—as though nothing bad could happen ever again in the world. It smelled of grain and of harness dressing and of axle grease and of rubber boots and of new rope. And whenever the cat was given a fish-head to eat the barn would smell of fish. But mostly it smelled of hay, for there was always hay in the great loft up overhead. And there was always hay being pitched down to the cows and the horse and the sheep.
> *Charlotte's Web*, E. B. White, 13

When we reverse ratiocinate this particular text, we focus on this sentence, "It often had a sort of peaceful smell—as though nothing bad could happen ever again in the world." It's important to discuss how the em—dash allows a writer to briefly shift the tone of his or her piece. The change that my students have shown using this tool almost acts as a thought shot. They not only learned how an em—dash is utilized grammatically, but also how one enriches the general feeling of their texts. Some of my students inserted an em—dash into their writing to create a change in tone:

> All the goodbyes had been said expect to my bestie. I asked my grandma if we could call or stop by her house but she replied, "Only if you want to lose time." I said, "no"—but I really did want to lose time.

The Part Where We Shift—like this...

We had a big party for Jaci's '0' birthday in the hospital—just like they did for me when I was born.

My dad's friend dared him to drink alcohol—I begged him not to.

You don't really need a big turtle—you just need the right pet and some love.

I was not a happy camper anymore—I was an unhappy camper.

We put her in the hole and they were about to put the dirt on her. I ran over to the hole and said, "Dad, wait!" I stared at her—it was the selfish part of me that just wanted her back.

Chapter Seven: Revertiocination

The Part Where It Goes On Forever

Surely there are millions of passages in the literary world that can contribute to the strategy of reverse ratiocination. I read them daily and I dream about using them in the context of the classroom. As the great John Irving once said, "Half my life is an act of revision." And what better way to pour a half-full cup than to continually revise how to revise.

Reverse ratiocination has been a whirlwind of discoveries and challenges and growth and moments of blissful insight. The voyage is certainly not complete, but I witness each day a harvest of minds invested to the point of no return.

REFERENCES:

Carroll, Joyce Armstrong, and Edward E. Wilson. *Acts of Teaching*: Second Edition. Portsmouth: Heinemann, 2008.
Dahl, Roald. *Matilda*. New York: Viking, 1988.
DiCamillo, Kate. *Because of Winn-Dixie.* Somerville: Candlewick, 2000.
Jiang, Ji-li. *Red Scarf Girl.* New York: Harpercollins, 1998
Rowling, J.K. *Harry Potter and the Sorcerer's Stone.* New York: Scholastic, 1999.
White, E.B. *Charlotte's Web.* New York: Harpercollins, 1952.
Wink, Joan and LeAnn Putney. *A Vision of Vygotsky.* Boston: Allyn & Bacon, 2001.

EMILY E. SMITH lives in Austin, Tx, and *lives* to teach. Growing up as the daughter of an Abydos trainer, Amy Jarvis Smith, her six years spent within the program have been crucial to her successes in the classroom. Emily is looking forward to applying to grad schools in the near future and continuing her relationship with Abydos Learning International.

At the 24th Annual Abydos Teachers' and Trainers' Conference, diamond trainer Becky Coker presented "Ratiocination: The Door to Grammar Cognition." Her session was standing-room-only with lots of interaction and lots of questions. That single session solidified for me the need for an in-depth book on the topic and Coker as one of the contributors. Below she shows how she opened "the doorway to her students' minds using sequenced grammar paired with focused ratiocination." Taking advantage of teachable moments, Coker proves "ratiocination is not a 10-step worksheet; it is a year of brain-based grammar and usage lessons encouraging cognition."

dr jac

Chapter Eight
Ratiocination in the High School Classroom

Becky Coker

Ratiocination in the high school classroom fits perfectly into the writing process and the skills-based curriculum. Across the country, schools are emphasizing skills-based curricula to produce independent learners. Ratiocination targets this goal. We as writing teachers must trust in the process and create the opportunities for student learning to occur deeply and permanently. We must give our students the tools that—with time and practice—will provide a sense of accomplishment and confidence that comes from the ability to solve problems independently. Ratiocination serves as the ultimate tool in delivering grammar within the writing process, providing flexibility and endless coding opportunities adaptable to any grammar lesson. In my classroom, ratiocination begins within the writing process during revision and editing. My students ratiocinate after they have completed prewriting and have chosen a piece to take through the process. This piece may be any type of writing, any genre, not just creative writing as some seem to think. Ratiocination is a powerful personal tool giving students control in their writing forever not just for one paper or a test.

Chapter Eight: Ratiocination in High School

How Does Ratiocination Work

After many days of exploring topics, my students generate at least five pieces of writing geared toward whatever is the curriculum-required genre at that time. After conferencing and thinking about the target goals, each student selects a piece that he or she will then use as the focus of instruction for the remainder of the writing process or unit. Normally, my students type their drafts, double-spacing them for ease in revision. Once we have a spell-checked copy, we begin ratiocination. My students often come to me with no ratiocination experience or only the experience of color coding followed by teacher directed instructions to "fix their weaknesses." Without decoding, ratiocination seems meaningless to them. We begin by highlighting the "to be" verbs. Often, if they see all ten codes, they want to move through all the coding strategies before addressing the needs of their first coding. Only one or two codes per paper works best.

With a list of "to be" verbs in hand, students begin highlighting or circling all the "to be" verbs in yellow. Empowered by this small success, my students aggressively seek out the vermin in their papers. Confident in their ability to do this, the room buzzes with activity. Then, I instruct the students to count the highlighted words, write the number at the top of the paper, and remove half. I instruct them to apply the "Decoding" information as they determine when to keep or change a "to be" verb. Again, they return to their papers with determination, but after five or ten minutes, they begin to flounder for solutions. BINGO! The optimal moment, the "Vygotskian" ZPD (Zone of Proximal Development) has arrived (Vygotsky, 189). They need solutions, and I have instruction—and plenty of modeling—to offer.

This is ratiocination in the classroom, the theory in practice. Ratiocination takes advantage of the ZPD and uses it as the key to teaching grammar in context. Teaching a grammar concept or revision strategy fulfills an immediate student need. Students will not be bored; they will not be confused; but they will be receptive to the solution for a problem that they have found in their papers. This is when grammar in context works. At this point appropriate grammar instruction occurs. The process is the same for any color coded clue although I am using the "to be" verb as an example.

The "to be" verb coding reveals weak areas, so I evaluate my students' needs

and teach a lesson designed to solve the problems I see in their papers. One such lesson is sentence combining, which offers solutions to many of the problems present in their papers and provides a framework for many different grammar concepts. So, we lay the papers aside and work on sentence combining.

What Happens Next

I use many of the sentence combining exercises in William Strong's *Sentence Combining: A Composition Book* (2nd ed). I introduce the strategy by using sentences on an overhead or white board—modeling the technique. For practice, I provide handouts of twenty to twenty-five related sentences. First, I model the process for the whole class; then they work with a partner on a sentence pair. We share. Next we double the group size and sentence numbers (four sentences instead of two). They share again. Confidence builds about the process and purpose of sentence combining. After much successful sharing and discussion about combining, I place a white sheet of butcher paper on the board to create an anchor chart of learning. Students debrief what they have learned during the process of sentence combining. They copy the anchor chart in their writing journals. An actual list of student debriefing appears on Chart A (Fig. 8.1).

Immediately, students use this new information and apply it to their own writing. They return to their papers and revisit the coded "to be" verbs. Now they have solutions to help them eliminate unnecessary "to be" verbs.

> **CHART A:**
> **Student Generated Agenda Chart for Sentence Combining:**
> - Meaning must remain the same.
> - Removing "be" verbs affects the surrounding sentences too.
> - Remove repeated words.
> - Create sentences with compound subjects and verbs.
> - Combine sentences using lists.
> - Turn describing sentences into adjectives or participles and place by object it describes in another sentence.

Fig 8.1

CHAPTER EIGHT: RATIOCINATION IN HIGH SCHOOL

IMPLICATIONS FOR TEACHING

Sentence combining offers practice in reducing clutter and creating more complex sentences. It offers one of the solutions possible for changing passive sentences into active as well as forcing students to "show not tell." Another benefit is creating familiarity with a strategy often presented on standardized tests. Caveat: Although sentence combining is an excellent strategy, students need to know that combining sentences is not always the best choice. Students must weigh the options available for clarifying meaning in an efficient but appropriate and fluent manner. The "decoding" information in Carroll's original article (1982), must be considered before a choice is made on whether or not the "to be" verb should or should not be removed. This list gives the student guidance in choosing which "to be" verbs to keep or replace.

SKILLS ADDRESSED:

- Sentence combining
- Adjectives
- Participles and Gerunds
- Compound Sentences
- Subordinate Clauses

Punctuation and Sentence Structure Minilesson
with "To Be" Verb Code

Coding "to be" verbs creates many opportunities for relevant lessons. Punctuating sentences properly is another such lesson. In this lesson, the focus is on correctly punctuating sentences using commas, semi-colons, and periods.

Punctuation and Sentence Structure Minilesson

MATERIALS

- Student writing
- Writing journal
- Comma pattern sheet
- Highlighters of 3 colors
- FANBOYS fan

PROCESS

Students take out their writing journals and the sentence/comma pattern sheet (Fig. 8.2) adapted from Carroll and Wilson's *Acts of Teaching* (2008). Then they locate the page for sentence/comma patterns in their writing journals.

BASIC COMMA PUNCTUATION IN SENTENCES

1. A COMPOUND SENTENCE must have a comma and FANBOYS or be punctuated with a semicolon alone to be correct. A comma alone is wrong.

SENTENCE [FANBOYS] SENTENCE

2. A LIST OR ITEMS IN A SERIES — Items in a list are separated by commas.

SENT   EN   [FANBOYS]   CE

3. INTRODUCTORY STUFF — Any word, phrase, or clause that comes at the beginning of the sentence, should be followed by a comma.

WORD, PHRASE, OR CLAUSE   MAIN SENTENCE

4. Unnecessary or Extra Information IS SURROUNDED BY COMMAS.

MAIN SEN-   WORD, PHRASE, OR CLAUSE   TENCE

Fig. 8.2

Chapter Eight: Ratiocination in High School

Next, students are instructed to list observations about the sentence/comma patterns using the Carroll/Wilson graphic. They do this for about ten minutes. At the end of ten minutes while the teacher acts as recorder, the students share observations and create a list on the board. It usually goes something like this:

Student/Teacher Conversation

Teacher:: Look at the comma pattern sheet. What do you notice?

Student: There are only four patterns.

Teacher:: Okay, what else? Describe the form without looking at the words.

Student: Well, there are boxes around stuff.

Teacher:: What stuff?

Student: Sentences and parts of the sentences, and they're separated by commas.

Teacher:: What do you think that means?

Student: Well, some are sentences by themselves, but others have to be added together to make one sentence.

Teacher:: So, we have boxes with the word "sentence" inside and something else. What's another element present in the comma patterns?

Student: Punctuation. I see commas, a semi-colon, and periods.

Teacher:: Good, now what else?

Student: One of the patterns has "FANBOYS" in the middle of it. Aren't those conjunctions?

Teacher:: Yes. Does anyone know anything about FANBOYS?

Student: For, And, Nor, But, Or, Yet, So, they are conjunctions you can use between sentences, right?

Teacher:: You're right, but remember they must have a comma before them in a compound sentence or it is wrong. Commas are never strong enough alone to place between two sentences, but with one of the FANBOYS, the punctuation is correct. See the pattern. What else about the commas in the other sentences? What do you see?

Student: "Unnecessary Information" has commas before and after.

Teacher:: So what can you conclude from that?

Student: I guess you don't really need that information for the main sentence, Right?

Teacher:: Right! Unnecessary information is often an appositive or an nonrestrictive clause that explains or defines the noun or concept before it. Good job! What about the introductory information?

Student: It has a comma after it and says, word, phrase, or clause, so I guess it always is set off with a comma.

Teacher: Great thinking! So let's review, what we have observed about the comma patterns:

CHAPTER EIGHT: RATIOCINATION IN HIGH SCHOOL

- There are 4 comma patterns.
- Boxes indicate structures like a sentence or non-sentence element.
- A comma comes before a FANBOYS when it separates two sentences.
- Commas go between items in a series if there are more than two.
- Commas set off introductory structures.
- Commas set off unnecessary information from the rest of the sentence

Teacher: Using three highlighting colors create a visual pattern in your writing journal of the sentence/comma patterns as they appear on the comma pattern chart. Next, label the sections correctly.

Students work in their journals using their writing.

Fig. 8.3

Code + Clue = Problem
Problem + Instruction = Solution
Cognition
Solution + Action = Revision
Revision x Practice = Learning
∴ Ratiocination = Learning

Fig. 8.4

Teacher: Look at your re-creation of the sentence and comma patterns in your journal. Did you punctuate the patterns correctly? If not, correct and then move on to the next step. Using your own writing, find an example of each of the sentence/comma patterns and write it in your journal under the correct sentence pattern. Use the highlighters to code these sentences in the same way as the patterns in your journal. Finally, let's create a quick tool to use with all your writing. (Teacher hands out blank mini-fans of seven strips of colored paper stapled or affixed with brad. See figures 8.3 and 8.4.) Using the blank multi-color fan, write each of the FANBOYS on one side. Next, turn over the fan and transfer one comma pattern to one strip on the back side of the fan. Label the parts as on the chart. Return to your paper and refer to the sentence/comma patterns as you combine

your own sentences, add proper punctuation, and reduce the "to be" verbs in your paper.

IMPLICATIONS FOR TEACHING

Repeated use of writing journals, manipulatives, graphics, and skills reinforce learning and offer models for future self-editing or peer editing. The repetitive nature of these tasks helps to create long-term memories of solutions for different writing problems. With the interconnected strategies, students experience logical scaffolding and concept building—discovering meaning as they go. Very Vygotskian right? Now students have solutions recorded in their writing journals for future reference. The process uncovers the logic behind ratiocination and makes the steps look deceptively simple.

SKILLS ADDRESSED

- Sentence Structure
- Comma Usage
- Run-on Sentences
- Comma Faults
- Comma Splice
- Parallel Structure
- Appositives
- Standardized test questions

More "To Be" Verb Lessons

Writing with your students if very important. I find my students think it is important, if I think it is important. I write every time my students write; therefore I have examples of every type of mistake and genre of writing. Often, I use my writing as models for them. This shows them that writing must be revised even for an English teacher.

Chapter Eight: Ratiocination in High School

Coker's model CHUNK #1

When I was a kid, I was fascinated with horses. I never owned one, but I read every horse book that was in the library. I even dug into the school garbage to find horse books that the library threw out. I found *Smoky the Cow Horse, Red Horse Hill, Windyfoot, King of the Wind*, and a lot of old books from around the turn of the century, but I never found my favorite horse books by Walter Farley, *The Black Stallion*. I loved them. I read every one and knew every flexing muscle of every Arabian horse in his books.

Whole Class Strategy

Revision

Use Chunk #1 and remove the "to be" verbs by combining the sentences or changing words, but do not change the meaning.

The Process

- Read chunk #1 aloud.
- Rewrite the sentences that have "to be" verbs.
- Combine sentences, but keep the original meaning.
- Record several samples and have students decide which retains the original meaning.

Invite students to share their revisions. The final revision will look something like this. Post for all to see.

REVISED SENTENCE

As a child, horses fascinated me. Since I never owned a horse, I read every library book on horses that I could find.

What did we do? (Record on board or poster as students brainstorm.)

- Changed "when I was a kid" to a prepositional phrase: "As a kid."
- Made the subject "horses" and the verb "fascinated": "horses fascinated me."
- Reduced "every book that was in the library" to an adjective: "library book."

CHECK PUNCTUATION

Revisit the comma patterns and add punctuation.

Pair Up and Practice:
COKER'S MODEL CHUNK #2

I started collecting ceramic horses that looked like the ones in the Walter Farley books. My first purchase for $1.00 was the Flame. It was a perfect palomino with one white-stocking foot raised and its mane blowing in the wind. I put it on my dresser, so I could see it whenever I was in the room. Everyone knew it was special.

- Read chunk #2 silently and discuss with each other how to remove the "to be" verbs.
- Combine the sentences, but keep the original meaning.
- Rewrite the revised sentence on white boards or sentence strips.
- Keep the original meaning.
- Students show their sentences when teachers says "Show" not before.

Chapter Eight: Ratiocination in High School

Invite students to share their revisions. The final revision will look something like this. Post for all to see.

Completed Paragraph Revision

> I started collecting ceramic horses that looked like the ones in the Walter Farley books. I purchased my Flame, a perfect palomino, for a $1.00 in 1961. Frozen in motion with its mane blowing in the wind, the Flame still raises one white-stocking foot as if it has just stopped in full gallop to check the horizon for danger. I placed it on my dresser, so I could see it whenever I entered the room. Everyone knew I loved it.

What did we do? (Continue to record on board or poster as students brainstorm.)

- Changed first sentence from passive to active using "I purchased" instead of "was purchased."
- Reduced "It was a perfect palomino" to an appositive and placed after "my Flame."
- Added the word "Frozen to replace "It was" and added the rest of the sentence.
- Replaced "was in the room" with "entered" an action verb.
- Replaced the last "was special" with "I loved it."

Stop and Reflect

Once the students have discussed the sentences, they should choose the one that does the best job and keeps the original meaning. Next, we test it for validity.

- Have you eliminated the "to be" verbs?
- Does is read well when read aloud?
- Does it need punctuation?
- Are there unnecessary repeated words?
- Does the sentence still mean the same thing?

Independent Practice

Independent Practice

REVISION

Final teacher instructions help students activate and use their learning for their own writing. By using their own writing, students revisit the highlighted "to be" verbs. They revise and strengthen their writing by removing unnecessary "to be" verbs and use the comma pattern fan to help. Additionally, they consult their writing journals for information.

As the students find errors, they rewrite the revised sentences on a separate sheet of paper, numbering the newly combined sentences. Cross referencing with the same number in the original paper, the students write a number indicating the new sentence's placement. Each student continues evaluating each highlighted "to be" verb as a candidate for change. In the end, they may have removed more or less than half of the "to be" verbs, but their papers will be stronger, and they have learned to think, change, and evaluate the use of "to be" verbs by themselves.

ANCHOR CHART

- Two related sentences may be joined by a comma and "FANBOYS" (coordinating conjunction).
- Subordinate clauses may be used to reduce information and glue it to another sentence.
- Place a comma after introductory elements.
- Subordinate clauses function as parts of speech: adjectives, adverbs, or nouns.
- Descriptive sentences (passive sentences) can be reduced to adjectives or adjective phrases and placed in a nearby sentence next to the word they modify.
- Verbs can be turned into participial (adjective) or gerund (noun) phrases and placed in a nearby or new sentence as an adjective or noun.
- Time information may be reduced to prepositional phrases and added to a nearby sentence.

This is a good time to remind students that they should attach these new adjectives or adjective phrases in close proximity to the word being modified—

Cahpter Eight: Ratiocination in High School

often at the beginning of the sentence as an introductory element. Finally, students record the anchor chart in their writing journals for future use.

Implications for Teaching

By the end of this strategy, I have taught at least eight grammar concepts. This is Vygotsky, Brunner, and Dewey in the classroom. Ratiocination illuminates possible weaknesses, creating the need in the student for a solution. By creating the Vygotskian opening and building the Brunner scaffold with the large group, small group, and finally independent practice, ratiocination's logic gradually emerges through Dewey's experiential learning. This is ratiocination—independent thought in the classroom. With this practice, students move from pseudo-concepts through the process to genuine concepts. (Vygotsky 123). They become active learners.

Code: Underlining of Sentences in Alternating Colors.

Materials:

- Comma Pattern Sheet,
- Seven two inch by one half-inch slips of different colored paper stapled at one end
- Students' writing
- Two different colored highlighters

Process

Using the mini-fan from the prior lesson as a reminder of the coordinating conjunctions ("FANBOYS") and the correct punctuation for the four basic sentence patterns, students use two highlighters and underline their sentences in alternating colors. Each student closely examines each sentence making note of the color patterns. Is there a short block of color? If so, is it a fragment? Could it be joined to another sentence? Check the comma pattern. Make changes if necessary and move to the next sentence. Is there a large block of color? Check

the comma patterns. Could this be a compound sentence? Should it be broken into several sentences. Use the comma pattern fan to guide the changes. Students continue using these tools, moving through their paper as they match their sentences to one of the patterns and check the comma placement.

IMPLICATIONS FOR TEACHING

Strike while the iron is hot! That is another way of saying Vygotsky's "Zone of Proximal Development" must be utilized in order for instruction to be valid or useful. Therefore, once students have combined sentences eliminating "to be" verbs, they have need of punctuation for their new sentences. This also helps those who have not been successful on the first try to have multiple chances to learn a concept. Most students do not get it the first time. In my experience, ratiocination creates a logical sequence that makes more sense and offers hope for success. The ratiocination process is like a grammar crime scene investigation. That beats worksheets any day.

The teacher's planning and thought process for ratiocination in the classroom is very important. Ratiocination is not a worksheet to hand over to students to do for homework. As indicated in the lessons in this section, every code has many possibilities. This strategy generates questions that in turn generate answers covering many concepts in grammar, punctuation, and usage. Ratiocination is a universe of revision and grammar lessons. Think carefully about the needs of the students and plan accordingly. As many teachers discover very quickly, ratiocination is not limited to the original ten coding items; variations spontaneously arise out of student needs. This strategy, firmly rooted in brain and educational research, is a powerful process for teaching and creating independent, confident learners. As with learning, the possibilities of ratiocination never end. Even as I write this, I am planning new ways to use it in my classroom. In order to crystalize my vision of ratiocination and help me in my own planning, I have created a graphic that reminds me of the ratiocination process. Figure 8.5 is my graphic representation of ratiocination.

Fig. 8.5

> **Code + Clue = Problem**
> **Problem + Instruction = Solution**
> Cognition
> Solution + Action = Revision
> Revision x Practice = Learning
> ∴ Ratiocination = Learning

Chapter Eight: Ratiocination in High School

REFERENCES

Carroll, Joyce Armstrong. "Ratiocination and Revision, or Clues in the Written Draft." *English Journal* (November 1982), 90-92.

Carroll, Joyce Armstrong and Edward Wilson. *Acts of Teaching: How to Teach Writing*, 2d Ed. Westport, CT: Teacher Idea Press, 2008.

Strong, William. *Sentence Combining: A Composing Book* (2nd ed.). NY: Random House, 1973.

Vygotsky, Lev. *Thought and Language*. Translated and edited by Alex Kozulin. Cambridge, MA: 1986.

BECKY COKER has taught writing at both the middle school and high school level in Texas and Montana. Currently she teaches both sophomore and junior English at Bryan High School in Bryan, Texas. A graduate of Texas A&M University, with degrees in English and history, she first became a writing process teacher when she experienced the three-week New Jersey Writing Project (NJWPT) institute in June 1992. After almost twenty years of growing and learning in the writing process, Becky is still motivated by a passion for learning that she works to transfer to her students through experiential discovery based learning in the writing process classroom. Currently she holds the Diamond Level Trainer certification with ABYDOS International (formerly the NJWPT). In addition to her teaching, Becky is a wife and mother of a son and daughter and four glorious grandchildren.

Section Four
Other Voices

It would be wonderful to use all the variations on ratiocination that I received over the years and while writing this book, but space does not permit that luxury. In "Other Voices," I tried to cull from the potpourri of offerings several that illustrated the range and depth of ratiocination. Shirley Blanton uses it to teach tone to ninth-grade students, Sonja Edwards presents powerful proof that it helps her seventh-grade students realize that writing never ends, Jean Hawsey introduces figurative language to sixth-grade students through ratiocination, whereas Judy Wallis finds it supports the writing life on the post graduate level. These voices, coupled with the myriad examples found earlier in the book, show that with thoughtful planning teachers of all grade levels may use ratiocination to teach every grammatical and linguistic concept in their standards.

dr. jac

Chapter Nine
Ratiocination and Reading

Shirley Blanton

Why teach tone to kids? Tone is, after all, a difficult concept to master and students probably get along pretty well without knowing much about it other than to know a definition to pass a teacher-made test. Were it really that simple! No longer can tone be glossed over and just mixed together with mood while teachers and students move on to other "more important" things. Fortunately or unfortunately, depending on your viewpoint, we need to teach tone, for it becomes a springboard for teaching many literacy skills and reinforcing others.

Tone has been on state-mandated tests, although often in a simple format, and will appear on the upcoming End of Course Exams (EOC) being constructed for the state of Texas. So teaching tone through ratiocination improves reading skills and scores because it focuses students on words (vocabulary) and shows the importance of words to comprehension, thus giving teachers another way to address inference. Ratiocinating tone words opens the way to necessary lessons on connotation and denotation and deals with multiple meaning words as well as with words the students may not know or never bothered to define.

Ratiocinating tone affords the teacher an opportunity to provide oral practice in how to explain and prove a point, which is good practice for any open-ended response requiring analysis and commentary. Actually, working with tone is really fun because it allows students to think, speak, and share. As students work with tone, they begin to see that words, images, and sentences impact meaning plus they have another way to re-enter their own writing to make it stronger. Finally, students gain confidence in their ability to read with depth.

Chapter Nine: Ratiocination and Reading

Model Lesson

The following lesson is one that I have used for several years with my Pre-AP ninth-grade students. Please, do not roll your eyes and stop reading yet! I also used this lesson with regular ninth graders, and not so amazingly, the regular kids "got it" just about as quickly as my Pre-AP kids did.

So, please, read on, step into the world of tone, use the familiar revision technique of ratiocination, and empower your students to read deeply and with greater comprehension.

In order to start, you will need:

Supplies:
• Copies of the first two paragraphs of "The Scarlet Ibis" by James Hurst enlarged to allow students to mark their own copies.
• Markers
• Teacher copy of "The Scarlet Ibis" to use on overhead or projected on a screen; teacher needs markers or Vis-à-vis® pens in different colors.

Prior to lesson—Priming students and text

- Teacher shows pictures of a scarlet ibis, a bleeding tree, rural South Carolina in the early 1900's, phlox, a grindstone, an oriole.
- Discuss whether these items are attractive, unattractive, or neutral. ("Google • Images" is your friend.)
- Students read "The Scarlet Ibis" without first discussing the story

Days 1 and 2:

Reporting Categories

- Identifying tone; determining how tone is created
- Practicing explaining using academic thinking and organization

1. Give each student a copy of the first two paragraphs of "The Scarlet Ibis" along with two different colored markers;

2. Students read the two paragraphs out loud – use "popcorn" reading or another method for involving more than one student;

3. Ask the students what feeling or emotion they experienced or felt or noticed after the reading. (You will notice that about half the class did not feel anything or notice anything.) Some students will tell you that they felt sad or felt like something bad was going to happen.

4. Ask:

>Teacher: What made you feel sad or feel that something bad was going to happen.

They will say,

>Student: "Well, it's the way the writer writes."

If you ask them to be more specific, they may be at a loss. Why? Many young people who are not good readers just read words, possibly know definitions, but they do not really grasp the concept behind the words. Many of these are the readers who didn't feel or notice anything. Good readers often know and can infer tone but do not know how they know what they know. Both groups need help with understanding the impact of words and images on comprehension and enjoyment. Both groups need to understand tone---to recognize it in other people's writing and to use it as a tool in their own writing.

DIRECT TEACH ON TONE

1. Explain to students that any feelings they noticed when reading has to do with tone. Define tone as the author's attitude towards the subject or thing he/she is writing about or the author's attitude towards his/her audience. Help students understand that they should think of tone as an emotion or feeling that they notice during the reading. Students put this information in their notes or write the definition on their copies of the paragraphs. Some students will ask if authors use tone on purpose. If you get this question, be happy because it gives you an entrance into explaining that authors do this on purpose to manipulate the reader into seeing what the author wants the reader to see or to believe what the author wants the reader to believe. If no one asks this question, share this concept with

Chapter Nine: Ratiocination and Reading

the students.

2. Show students writers create tone through:
   Diction (another word for *words* or *vocabulary*),
   Images,
   Details,
   Language,
   and Syntax
   (DIDLS).

Students write this information in their notes or on their copies of the story. The **DIDLS** acronym comes from College Board workshops. Because learning needs to be scaffolded, explain that, right now, they will be working with **Diction** and **Images**. Trying to do everything at once is counter productive.

3. Ask the students :

   Teacher: What is the tone of these two paragraphs?

They will chorus:

   Students: sad.

If half the class offers another tone, and half gives you *sad*, vote. It is much easier for the students at this point to work with *sad* or *melancholy* or *mournful* than it is to work with *regretful*. Remind them that they want an emotion or feeling.

4. Here ratiocination begins. Students code all the single words that strike them as sad or melancholy in the two paragraphs by circling the "sad" words in marker. Students work independently.

5.   Allow six to eight minutes for coding the words.

6.   Place the photocopy of the two paragraphs on the overhead or document camera and invite students to share the sad words in the first line. (It is best to work line-by-line because you are going to use this coding to help students learn how to explain their thinking.) Code your copy as the students offer words. Ask

Direct Teach on Tone

for an explanation why each word was coded; in other words, invite them to explain why a word struck them as sad, "to show their thinking," to use Tovani's phrase. (Student answers will usually be something like "Well, it's sad because death is sad.") This explanation is not satisfactory.

As Doug Lemov says, "Right is Right is about the difference between partially right and all-the-way right—between pretty good and 100 percent" (35).

7. Prod the student to explain why death is sad. Usually you will get something more like "death is an end and endings are sad because there is no more," or "death reminds me of my aunt who passed away last year." Model an appropriate "set up" for the answer: The word *death* is sad because death is the end of something and people grieve for the things that die or end. Have students explain using this format every time. Give high-fives and cheers when they explain correctly.

8. Continue with all the words. Do not accept a "sad" word without an explanation why the word is sad. If students miss a word that carries a sad connotation, point the word out and do a direct teach on symbolism. (Example: students never mark the word *autumn* as a sad word because they do not associate seasons with a life cycle. Explain this possible symbol to them and show them how this season is apt for the tone and for the purpose of this tone.)

9. Students count the *sad* words. Obviously, this strategy lets them see that the preponderance of words in the piece connect to something sad, reinforcing the concept that the tone here is one of sadness or melancholy.

10. Next have them take their other marker and code the images that seem to be sad by underlining them. Some sad words will appear in the images but that is all right. Allow six to eight minutes for the coding.

11. Moving line by line, volunteers share their sad images and explain why the image is sad using the format followed for words above. Change *word* to *image* of course. Continue high-fiving and cheering well-explained justifications.

12. After discussing the images (be sure to let more than one student explain why they think an image is sad; there are no carved in stone "right" answers and you want several ideas and you want many students to have the opportunity to

CHAPTER NINE: RATIOCINATION AND READING

practice explaining in a coherent way). Students count the images underlined.

> Teacher: Considering the number of words and images you underlined, what would you say the tone of these two paragraphs is? How did you figure out that the tone the author used is sad or melancholy?

Usually, they will say some variation of

> Student: "By looking at the words and images."

13. Ask:

> Teacher: So, are words important to know what is going on? Are images important? Or are they just plunked in for fun?
>
> Teacher: Ok, so why did the author use this tone?

They will answer

> Student: "Because he wants you to feel sad."

Ask:

> Teacher: Why does he want you to feel sad?

If their reasoning is circular, they may not know that tone has a purpose.

14. Do a **direct teach** on the purpose of tone. Tone connects to theme, to character development, to foreshadowing, to symbol. If students have read the story, they will see immediately that the tone foreshadows the death of Doodle, so they have had a concrete lesson that tone can foreshadow an outcome. In the past, I have had many students who read "The Scarlet Ibis" and didn't realize that Doodle dies at the end. It took ratiocinating the two paragraphs at the beginning to convince them that he was abandoned (clearly illustrated in the opening paragraphs) and

Direct Teach on Tone

that he died (mentioning *dead* more than once is a clue).

15. Stop here and go to another short piece of literature and repeat this lesson OR move to writing about tone in a literary analysis OR move to the lesson changing tone from sad to happy or cheerful. Figure 9.1.

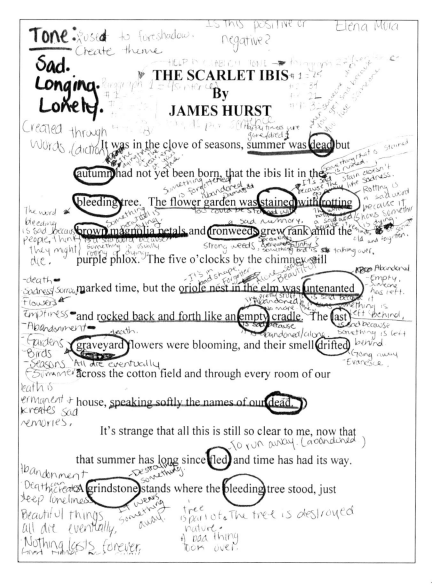

Fig. 9.1

Chapter Nine: Ratiocination and Reading

Day 3:
Changing tone and the impact of sentence structure on tone

1. Students pair up; either assign pairs or allow students to choose.
2. They re-write the two paragraphs changing the sad or melancholy words and images to cheerful, bright, happy words and images. Allow class time for this strategy. Encourage use of a thesaurus. Expect talking; encourage it.
3. Ask for volunteers to share their new paragraphs. Have more than one group to share. Post the paragraphs. Figures 9.2 and 9.3.

> **Making "Scarlet Ibis" Happy**
>
> It was in the clove of seasons, summer was alive but fall has not yet been born, that the ibis lit in the healthy tree. The flower garden was beautiful and alive with red magnolia petals and green amid the purple phlox. The grass grew by the chimney still marked time and the five o'clocks oriole nest like a baby cradle in the elm was filled with little chirping birds. The garden flowers were blooming, and their smell floated across the cotton field and through every room of our house, speaking softly.
>
> It's strange that all this is still so clear to me, now that the summer has long since begun, and time has had its way. A blooming tree stands where the grindstone stood, just outside the kitchen door, and now if an oriole sings in the elm, its song seems to rise up in the leaves. The flower garden is prim, the house a gleaming white, and the brown fence across the yard stands straight and spruce. But sometimes (like right now), as I sit in the cool, green-draped parlor, the wheel begins to turn, and time with all its changes is worned away --- and I remember Doodle.

Fig. 9.2

Changing Tone

> **Ray Tafolla & Laois Sumrall:**
>
> **Making Scarlet Ibis Happy.**
>
> It was in the clove of seasons, summer was poppin' but spring had not yet been ban, that the Ibis lit in the dancing tree. The flower garden was pretty with vibrant white, magnolia petals and dandelions grew uncontrabally amid in the purple phlox. The five o'clocks by the chimney still marked time, but the oriole nest in the elm was full of life and rocked back and forth like a baby cradle. The first greenhouse flowers were blooming, and their smell loomed across the cotton field and through every room of our house, speaking softly the names of the newban.
>
> It's strange that all this is still so clear to me, now that summer has since began, and time has yet to have its way. A little boy climbs where the dancing tree stands, just outside the kitchen door, and now if an oriole sings in the elm, it's song seems to cascade up in the leaves, a silvery shine. The flower garden is prim, the house a gleaming white, picket fence across the yard stands straight and spruce. But sometime (like right now), as I sit in the cool, green draped parlor, the grandpappy clock begins to turn, and time with all its changes are shaken like a polaroid picture --- and I chill with lil' Doodle.

Fig. 9.3

Chapter Nine: Ratiocination and Reading

4. At this time, you may look at the effects of sentence structure or you can stop here and go to another short piece of literature to repeat the lesson you have just done to reinforce the learning.

Day 4 or Later:
Reporting category—Looking at sentence structure
and its effect on tone

1. Pair students up using whatever method you choose. Half the pairs count the sentences in the first paragraph while half the pairs count the sentences in the second paragraph of the original story. Ask for a report. Put this information on the board.

2. Keeping the pairs, half the students count the words in the sentences in the first paragraph while the other half count the words in the sentences in the second paragraph. Ask for a report. Put this information on the board.

3. Ask:

> Teacher: What do you notice about these sentences?
>
> Student: They are long.
>
> Teacher: Can you tell what kind of sentences the author used?

(You may have to teach or re-teach compound sentences since the preponderance of sentences fall into the compound category. This is an excellent time to integrate grammar with the effect of sentence structure on tone.)

> Teacher: What is the effect of these compound sentences? What do they do to the reader?

The students may say they are boring. You might want to change that word to *plodding* or *slow* or *languid*.

Sentence Structure and its Effect on Tone

> Teacher: Why would the author write such long, slow sentences in these two paragraphs?

You want to get the students to think about a funeral procession and how slowly it moves or to think about how slowly grief leaves people after a death or how when a person is depressed, he/she feels like he/she is unable to move. The sentences, because they are long, help to create the sad, melancholy tone.

4. Now, they re-read their "happy" paragraphs.

> Teacher: Even with the words and images changed, do your paragraphs "feel" happy?

The answer should be no, because they have such long sentences.

5. Students, in their own words, add to their notes that long sentences are explanatory, slow, serious, and academic. Short sentences add drama or suspense and are used to startle the reader or make a dramatic point. They move the reader quickly and increase tension.

6. Show the students a skeleton paragraph. Figure 9.4.

> I was walking down the street after breaking up with my fiancé. I was thinking of how sad I was to have lost my love. He was the person I thought I'd spend the rest of my life with. I heard a sound behind me. I was alone. I was a little scared. I turned around. I couldn't see anything behind me so I walked on. I heard the sound again. It was a little sound . I stopped and waited. That's when I saw the little black and white kitten. It looked at me. I walked to it . I saw that it was dirty and really thin. I spoke to it. It came to me meowing. I picked it up and told it that since we were both alone that I'd take it home. That's how I found a new friend and became happier.

Fig. 9.4

CHAPTER NINE: RATIOCINATION AND READING

Ask the students if they liked the piece. Their answers will be negative even derogatory, which you want. Ask students to identify the tone of that paragraph. This they easily. Separate the piece into three parts and put students into groups. Give each group one section. You will have more than one group working each section. Have them create tone by adding appropriate diction, images, and sentences. Figures 9.5, 9.6. 9.7. Students present their work and explain what they added and why.

> I was walking down the street after breaking up with my fiancé. I was thinking of how sad I was to have lost my love.
>
> He was the person I thought I'd spend the rest of my life with.
>
> Yazmin C.
> Josh H.
> Christian R.
>
> *Keying*
>
> I was walking down the alley after breaking up with my fiancé, I tought of evil things I could do to get back at him, like slashing his tires or keeing his car. After all she cheated on me with my best friend. Who am I to think he was going to be the Love of my Life? Why do terrible things happen to good people like me for no reason? Does he not understand that he broke my heart?

Fig. 9.5

Student Rewrites

Angie   Travis   Erik   Gabby

I heard a sound behind me. I was alone. I was a little scared. I turned around. I couldn't see anything behind me so I walked on. I heard the sound again. It was a little sound. I stopped and waited.

I heard a faint scratching sound behind me. Since I was alone in the eerie darkness of an alley, I was terrified. I turned around to find the source of the sound, but there was no one out there but me. Just me. I quickened my pace. When I heard the sound again, I froze. Paralyzed by fear.

Fig. 9.6

CHAPTER NINE: RATIOCINATION AND READING

Jose
Lexi

That's when I saw the little black and white kitten. It looked at me. I walked to it. I saw that it was dirty and really thin. I spoke to it. It came to me meowing. I picked it up and told it that since we were both alone that I'd take it home. That's how I found a new friend and became happier.

That's when I saw the loney little black and white kitten. It glared at me with big brown depressing eyes. I moved towards it. I saw that it was dirty and very thin. As I whispered to the kitten it crawled towards me. with a limp on his left front leg meowing. I scooped it up and gave it a comforting hug. I spoke to it softly, saying I was going to nurse this poor kitten back to health. That's when I realized the kitty was just like me, alone and helpless, we were a perfect match for each other. My new friend made me much happier and healed the wound from the broken heart of my ex-fiance.

Lexi and Jose
4th

Fig. 9.7

A Little More
Reporting Category—Students Re-enter Their Own Writing

1. Students find one place in something they have already written where they could create tone. They box the location in their writing.

2. On a separate sheet of paper, they revise their writing by developing tone using better words, strong images, and appropriate sentence structure.

FINALLY!

I have always like to debrief with students about a lesson or an assignment to see how they felt the lesson affected their learning. I was gratified to find that the students enjoyed this lesson, even though in places they struggled.

Trevor stated, "I have never learned about sentence structure affecting tone until now, and I understand it."

Angie, who stated that she didn't like to be called on because she was shy, said, "…when we had to circle the underline words and phrases in the two paragraphs, I began to understand tone a little more clearly."

Kaylee had a similar epiphany. She wrote," It showed me that words and the way you write your sentences are very important. I learned that by having long sentences and placing a few short ones in between it creates sespenc [sic]—a must have in writing interesting stories."

Angel wrote that circling "the words helped me understand tone and how its [sic] created."

Mauricio shared, " Circling the sad words of the first two paragraphs helped me understand tone a lot more. The circling with markers made it easier to understand. If you could do that for everything you teach, it would sure make a difference."

Chapter Nine: Ratiocination and Reading

Ratiocination is a fantastic tool for helping writers revise. However, it is also a useful tool in helping students read and understand because it makes concepts stand out. I think Mauricio said it best: "If you could do that (circle and underline) for everything, it would sure make a difference." I hope this lesson will give you a place to start in thinking about using ratiocination in both literature and writing. Reading for tone can be difficult, but students can be successful if given the tools to attack this difficult concept. Those tools can be as simple as looking at words, images, and sentence length.

Shirley Watts Blanton has spent forty years teaching somebody something. Thirty of those years were spent teaching grades sixth through twelfth and functioning as English Department chairperson in three high schools. In 1991 her teaching life really began when she attended an NJWPT institute which caused her to re-think all that she had been doing. In actuality, the institute caused her to start thinking about how to help students learn. She is a Diamond Level trainer with Abydos and has had articles and poetry published in *English in Texas* and in *R&E Journal*. Retired now, she presents in-services and workshops to help teachers improve writing instruction.

Chapter Ten
Successful Revision Demands Writer's Discretion

Sonja Edwards

My favorite thing to do with students' writing early in the year is to slowly introduce the idea that we are never really finished with writing. We talk about the recursive process that they somewhat understand; we have "process snakes" hanging above our heads reminding us that we can always go back into any piece and prewrite, write, edit, and revise. But why would we do that? Students tire of hearing this quote from me: "Our writing can always get better!" I like to have them see what I mean.

By seventh grade, students have had many writing opportunities, but they may not have had many revision opportunities. With this a high stakes year in writing, my English classes are busy putting pens and pencils to work. Each day we write in our journals about various topics. By the end of the first six weeks, students have taken a selected piece and completed a personal narrative, which we have worked with to add depth. Then the day arrives when students rewrite their chosen writing into a final piece.

The due day for this final piece is usually quite stressful because students are just beginning to trust me with their feelings and emotions. Turning over this writing to me takes a great deal of faith. When they come in, I tell them to keep their writing because it is not quite complete. Immediately they ask if they are going to have to rewrite the paper after they mark on it; I smile. Ratiocination begins. Explaining that I want them to analyze what they have written, they stare with blank looks and open mouths, "What? How?"

I invite each student to go back and mark the end of each sentence—two

Chapter Ten: Successful Ratiocination

red vertical lines at each end punctuation mark. Figure 10.1 below. Next, we go back and circle in green the first word of each new sentence. (This alone offers numerous teaching moments.)

Fig.10.1

Sample Student Work

After we mark the papers, I simply ask, "What do you notice?" Conversation immediately goes to the following: long sentences (maybe run-ons), short sentences (maybe fragments), many marks the same length apart, many vertical lines (students start counting and comparing), fewer vertical lines (again comparison), same green circled word, the list goes on—and I let it!

Right or wrong, I write all comments on the board and say very little. I have learned that during this first interaction with our newborn text, students need to be allowed to delicately handle it and assess its newness without my dictation. (In past years, unfortunately, I tried to monitor and force students to notice things, which killed the conversation. Then—I was judging their babies.) If they share ideas willingly without my input, students don't feel threatened. The conversation and the environment have to create a sense of success; anything a writer chooses is right if it works for the purpose established. Therefore, I try to be very sensitive, joining in the conversation to help students justify writing choices in order to build their confidences. I let the students be amazed at the level of conversation taking place after they have written their 'final piece' and have already claimed, "No, I don't need to change anything."

If the class is new and still feels sensitive about changing their works, they put the papers in their drafts folders to revisit at another time. No pressure. No stress. No rewriting—yet! Later, during ratiocination, minilessons and teacher facilitation occurs. We might look at changing first words or rearranging sentences, but for the first experience, because they often feel sensitive and inadequate, I want my writers to see what they have and determine where we can go.

If they see changes that will improve the stories, I encourage them to try the changes now. I go ahead and teach a minilesson, giving time to try out a strategy. Still no pressure. No stress. Just safe rewriting.

Once comfortable, we trust ourselves, and each other, to seriously critique our stylistic choices. We know that only then we will be able to make progressive changes.

Progressive changes that have moved us from, "Why revise?" to "Which revisions?" Getting thoughts down on paper the first time is one thing; it is not the only thing. Although this step provides comfort and control for the writer, the remainder of the process must not be overlooked. Going beyond the student's control as a writer, stepping out of his/ her safety net, the writing must be seen with the readers' eyes. Receive the writing as the reader would. *Have I emphasized what matters most? Do they understand that message?* The critical

Chapter Ten: Successful Ratiocination

moment comes when students analyze revisions as both reader and writer, and with confidence stand firm that each word, every punctuation mark, all sentences contribute to the piece as a whole. Sure, they may look back on the piece a week or so later and catch imperfections, but at the time of publishing, if the conveyed message is evident, they have achieved their purpose. *I revised with discretion; my reader received me.*

Classroom Conversation I

The following is a sample conversation my class and I might have as we look at the lengths of sentences in our drafts, trying to determine specific purposes for structure choices.

Reporting Categories:

to revise wording by looking at sentence variety and word choice

Key Terms:

recursive, process, revision, sentence structure, fragment, simple sentence, compound sentence, complex sentence, run-on

> Teacher: Everyone will need a red map pencil and a green map pencil. You will also need to have your developed draft on your desk and nothing else.
> Now I would like you to take your red map pencil and draw two vertical lines right after each end punctuation mark. (I model this using my own paper and give time for students to go through their entire pieces.)
> What do you notice when you look at your first page?

> Students: I have ten on the first page! (Surprise)
> What? I have two! (Laughter)
> I have five.

Classroom Conversation

              I have sixteen!
              Un-uh! Let me see.

Teacher: (This becomes like a competition, of course, because we are middle schoolers. Everyone begins calling out his or her numbers, and I wait.) What does this mean?

Students: (Silence, which shows thinking.) Well, maybe someone who only has two might have run-ons. Maybe the people who have a lot only have short-choppy sentences!
          Yea—or fragments!

Teacher: Ok. But what else might long sections indicate?

Students: Better sentences, more advanced writing.

Teacher: Yes. Long sentences are not always run-ons. We have to search to see if we have complex sentences or even compound-complex. It is ok to have advanced sentences in our papers.
    Sometimes that can slow down time if you are trying to build suspense.

Students: Oh.
    See I knew mine was ok. (Guilty person with only two gets justification.)

Teacher: Now, let's look at the other extreme. Who had the most marks?

Students: (Excitedly students shout out to determine the most. In our case, the person with sixteen.)

CHAPTER TEN SUCCESSFUL RATIOCINATION

Teacher: What might it mean if you have sixteen sentences on one page?

Students: My sentences might be fragments.

Teacher: Yes, that is true, but it could also mean...

Students: You were playing with time. Short choppy sentences could indicate past-paced action, movement.

Teacher: Another possibility is that your character is using his/her voice. What age of character might talk in short, choppy sentences?

Students: A kid! Or an old person, like my great-aunt at the nursing home! She doesn't talk much.

Teacher: Ok, so see. Sentences come in all lengths, all shapes, and all sizes. You, the writer, determines the right length for each sentence, not just for one or two, but for all.
   At this point I want you to go over the sentences on your first page or two with a partner to identify what type of sentence you have in each of your chunks. Label them as follows:

S-simple   F- fragment   RO- Run-on
CP- compound CX- complex

With your partner, talk about the purpose of these sentences and your choices. Do you need to fix anything? Should you turn the fragments into clauses?

Classroom Conversation

Give lots of time for student discussion and revision. After they master this process with a partner and are comfortable with identification, the rest of the writing may be completed independently.

Figure 10.1 shows a student who started his paper with a run-on. His corrections are marked.

Classroom Conversation II

Here students evaluate the first words in sentences for the first time.

> Teacher: Take your green map pencil and circle the first word of every sentence. These should be easy to find, why?

> Students: Because we have all end punctuation stopped by two vertical lines.

> Teacher: Correct, so go to all your vertical lines and circle the next word.

Give time for students to do this. Some papers are longer than others, so once a student is finished and waiting, this is the perfect time to look over the end marks and talk about a sentence or two with students, encouraging them to continue making decisions, changing, revising, etc.

> Teacher: When everyone is finished, I would like you to get notebook paper and write every circled word, like a list down the margins. Start with the left margin on the front side, then the right margin. If needed, move to the back and use those margins but leave the middle open.

> Students: I have a lot of *The's*
> I used *I* a bunch!

Chapter Ten: Successful Ratiocination

>Teacher: Hold on. We will discuss this in a moment. Everyone write the words down.

Students continue working, grinning, sometimes whispering to their neighbor about their overuse of a specific word

>Teacher: I would like you to read your list to your neighbor.
>Students: I, I, Then, We, He, I, The, There. . .
>He, He, He, He. . .

>Teacher: Let's talk about what you noticed.

>Students: I used the word *I* a whole bunch!

Naturally, again, students will start comparing numbers, so we go ahead and count.

>Teacher: Count how many times you repeated your most frequently used word.

>Students: I used *I* twelve times.
>*The* was my first word eight times.
>My sentences start with *Then* five times.
>I used *and* six times.
>*I* is my first word fifteen times.

Figure 10.2 shows a student who started his first four out of five sentences with *the*, which shocked him when he realized his first word crime.

>Teacher: What does this mean? Is it bad or good?

>Students: Well, I think it can get boring to have the same word at the start of each sentence.
>I thought we weren't supposed to start sentences with FANBOYS (coordinating conjunctions: for, and, nor, but, or, yet, so)
>Yea.

192

Classroom Conversation

Teacher: Well, that depends. Have you seen the Junie B. Jones books?

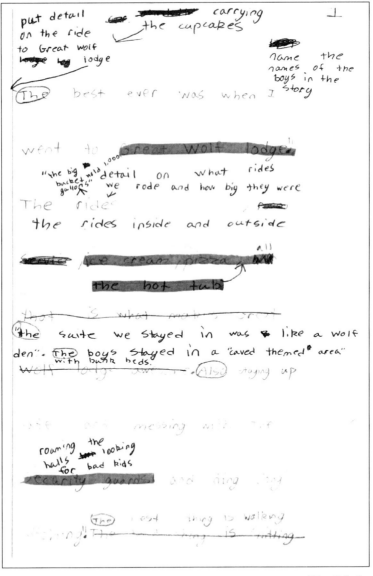

Fig.10.2

Chapter Ten: Successful Ratiocination

Students: Yes.

Teacher: Junie B. uses *and* many times to start sentences. Do you know why?

Students: That's how she talks.

Teacher: Right, she is a kindergartener. Those little ones do that often, so Barbara Park, the author, writes in a kindergarten voice. You have learned not to start with FANBOYS when you are writing in formal English. If you want to show voice in your stories, as long as you are not supposed to be writing a formal paper, you may start sentences with words like and. Sometimes doing that helps to build a character. Just be sure you know why you do what you do.

Students: Like in my book: they always have *but* at the beginning. I guess because they want shorter sentences.

Teacher: Right. You have to determine your audience and purpose. You have to decide how you are going to create an interesting character and how the sentences will build that character because most of the time your words are your readers' only pictures.

Students: How can you change it though? I don't want *the* eight times.

Teacher: Give me two of your *The* sentences and let's look at them together. Let's see if we can come up with this as a class.

Classroom Conversation

Write the examples and have students help rearrange the words or rewrite the sentences. Would that work in your story if we said it this way? (If yes, good. If no, listen to the author and try again.)

>Teacher: I would like everyone to have the opportunity to try reworking some sentences. Let's use the middle of the paper where we have space by our lists. Write two sentences that start with the same word--one at the top, one in the middle. Now, alone or with a partner, rework these sentences. See what you come up with. Warning: Don't substitute your repeated word for another repeated word. In other words don't change I to we if you have already used we a lot. Go for new words! (Allow time to work; walk around and offer assistance if needed. The driving force of these lessons is to allow ownership and to build confidence in these writers. Eventually these habits will flow naturally as works are produced! Practice.)

Figure 10.3 shows the student realizing that she had started several sentences with *so*, one of the FANBOYS, but she also realized her sentences were strong without it!

CHAPTER TEN: SUCCESSFUL RATIOCINATION

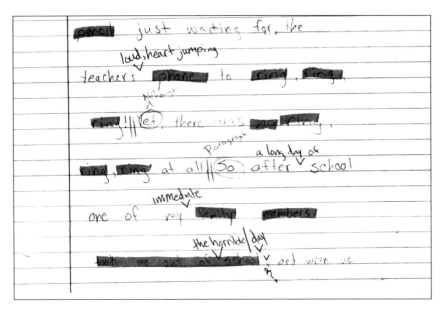

Fig.10.3

Your conversations may develop on a completely different level and your students may take other paths-- hurray! That is what keeps class fun! Just stay to the purpose. Empower the writer, giving meaning to each lesson, and praise success. Ratiocination will electrify writing. Go for it!

SONJA EDWARDS is in her 16th year as an educator. The first half of those years she enjoyed teaching full time in the elementary classroom. Her third and fourth graders challenged her and she, them. How could things be any more satisfying? Then, after a few years, she embarked on two new journeys: motherhood and middle school. What a combination! In a unique situation, she has the best of both worlds as she works in the classroom part time encouraging 7th grade writers. The other "part time" she enjoys spending with her children at home and running around. Her motto in both is "Play hard & have fun! Learn all you can along the way!" Sonja Edwards teaches in Alvord ISD.

Chapter Eleven
Figurative Language Meets Ratiocination

Jean Ewer Hawsey

Colorful Strategies for Ratiocination of "To Be" Verbs

To use "be" or not to use "be"—we know the answer to that question. Joyce Armstrong Carroll and Edward E. Wilson convinced us years ago that "to be" verbs are definitely not where the action is! One of the most important steps in ratiocination is the circling of those lackluster little verbs, but the task of replacing them with action verbs can be overwhelming. This very challenge inspired me to create some verb-revision strategies for my sixth-grade students. A fun game of "Verb Charades" introduces the forms of "to be" and brings home the importance of using vivid action verbs. "Similes in Action!" and "Personification Ratiocination" provide two strategies for weeding out "to be" verbs while also incorporating figurative language.

Play "Verb Charades" before using the simile and personification lessons. "Verb Charades" teaches the forms of "to be" and the importance of using action verbs to make writing more lively. This game gets students out of their seats and gives them a chance to unleash their "inner actors" while creating two lists on the board that show a clear contrast between action verbs and state of being verbs. At the end of the game, students clearly see why action verbs add excitement, movement, and imagery to their writing. Students are then ready to dive into their own pieces of writing, circle the forms of "to be," and begin the transformation.

"Similes in Action!" challenges students to remove "to be" verbs and create new sentences using *vivid action verbs* and *comparison*. The lesson also teaches the writing of similes and how similes add imagery to writing. "The runner *was* fast" becomes "The runner *took flight like a gust of wind*." Much better!

CHAPTER ELEVEN: FIGURATIVE LANGUAGE MEETS RATIOCINATION

"Personification Ratiocination" teaches personification while removing state-of-being verbs. This lesson works well with sentences whose subjects are inanimate objects (example: The tree was tall). Students target the verb they wish to remove (such as *was*) and brainstorm *human* actions the subject could perform. "The tree *was* tall" becomes "The graceful willow *reached* across the river." Personification replaces the "to be" verb with an action verb and also adds *life* to the writing. Students then move on to dabble with the addition of adjectives, adverbs, and descriptive phrases.

Writers cannot use similes and personification in *all* of the sentences they ratiocinate, but these two strategies invite them to transform at least a few of their sentences. If a student circles twenty "to be" verbs and has a goal of removing ten of them, the job is nearly half finished if he or she creates two new sentences with each of these lessons. Meanwhile, students will also hone their figurative language-writing skills.

VERB CHARADES

This is a fun strategy to do with your classes just before ratiocinating to remove forms of "to be" from students' writing. Often students do not see the difference between state-of-being verbs and action verbs, but they will after they play this game!

1. Cut 16 small strips of paper, approximately 1 inch X 2 inches or smaller.

2. Write one interesting action verb on each of 8 strips. Make sure each word represents an action that your students can "act out." Choose simple verbs such as *jump, cry, fall, dance, eat*, and so forth. Be sure to include at least one mental action such as *worry*.

3. On the remaining 8 strips, write the following forms of "to be": **am, is, are, was, were, be, being, been.**

4. Place only the **action** verbs together in a small container. Put the "to be" verbs aside until at least three or four students have acted out an action verb. The game

Verb Charades

will not have a fun beginning if students draw "to be" verbs and cannot act them out. Hold back these verbs until a few students have acted out action verbs.

5. Call on the first student to draw a verb. Ask the student to read the word silently and then act out the action, such as in a game of Charades.

6. Call on students (or allow the actor to call on students) to guess what action is being performed.

7. When a student correctly guesses the action verb, ask him or her to write the verb on the left-hand side of the board.

8. After at least four students have performed an action verb, drop the "to be" verbs into the container to be added to the drawing.

9. When a student draws a "to be" verb, he/she will not be able to act it out. Ask him or her to write the verb on the **right-hand side** of the board.

10. Continue until there are several verbs written in the left and right columns on the board. List all action verbs (physical and mental) on the left and state-of-being verbs on the *right*.

11. After all the verbs have been drawn (or when you have enough words on the board to examine), draw students' attention to the two lists of verbs.

Verbs	
fly	am
dance	is
sleep	are
crawl	was
cry	were
walk	be
worry	being
eat	been

CHAPTER ELEVEN: FIGURATIVE LANGUAGE MEETS RATIOCINATION

This is when the game turns into a teachable moment.

There are two lists of verbs before them, side by side. Ask students to look carefully at the two lists.

Remind them that they were able to "act out" all of the verbs on the left, but they were not able to show any action for the verbs on the right.

Take this opportunity to ask students how *worry* is different from the other action verbs. Students will answer that this action goes on in the mind. Explain that it is a mental action that you cannot see someone perform, but it is an action verb nevertheless. This presents an opportunity to discuss physical vs. mental actions. When your students debate that you *can* see a person worrying, point out that what they are actually seeing is the pacing, the nail-biting, or the intense facial expression, but that the actual *worrying* goes on in the mind, where no one can actually *see* it happening. This dialogue is worth your time because often, when students see a word representing a mental action such as "think," they do not realize that it is an *action* verb.

Ask students why they were unable to act out the verbs on the right. Students will most likely say, "They aren't things you can do" or "There is no action." Explain that the verbs on the right do not express action because they are forms of "to be" and can only express a state of **existence**, a state of **being** (or **condition**). Remind them of how much movement they saw when their classmates acted out the verbs from the list on the left side. Explain that this is because these verbs are action verbs and show a mental or physical action that a person or animal can **DO** (perform).

Now ask students which list of verbs will make their stories, essays, and poems more exciting and interesting for the reader. Students will immediately answer that the list of action verbs on the left is the winner and the "to be" verbs on the right will not put any pizzazz into their writing. Be sure to point out that vivid action verbs in their writing will paint a lively picture for the reader; the reader will be able to visualize the action. This will make students want to get rid of those boring, pesky little "to be" verbs!

Now that students have had some fun and understand why the state-of-being verbs do not help their writing come alive, they are ready for the ratiocination step of circling all of their "to be" verbs. Leave the lists of verbs on the board so that students can refer to them as they read through their own writing to find state-of-being verbs. Happy ratiocinating!

SIMILES IN ACTION!

The runner **was** fast.

The runner **took flight** *like a gust of wind*.

The use of simile is one of the best ways for a writer to *show* exactly what he or she wants the reader to see. When trying to eliminate a "to be" verb and replace it with an action verb, try using *comparison* to help express the idea in a new sentence.

Example 1: The coach **was** mad. (Target: eliminate *was*.)

A simile compares two *unlike* things, using the term *like* or *as*. Think of some things to *compare* the coach to when he is angry. What does he look like? How does he sound? How does he act? What can you compare him to? Show the reader an angry coach.

Think about the five senses as you write your similes. Choose a VIVID action verb, and think of a comparison.

Subject	Vivid Action	Comparison
The coach	exploded	like a firecracker
The coach's voice	boomed	like thunder
The coach's face	*turned	as red as a tomato
The coach	blew up	like a volcano
The coach's eyes	flashed	like red-hot flames
The coach	lashed out	like a fierce warrior in battle

*Although the verb "turned" is a linking verb, it conjures up an image of movement and change, unlike state-of-being verbs.

CHAPTER ELEVEN: FIGURATIVE LANGUAGE MEETS RATIOCINATION

Now create new sentences and decide which one creates the image you want your reader to see. You might even want to use more than one simile!

Example 2: The sun **was** hot. (Target: eliminate *was*.)

Subject	Vivid Action	Comparison
The sun	beat down upon us	like a blazing fire
The sun	pressed us	like a hot iron
The sun	burned	like a fiery explosion
The sun	heated the earth below	like a warm blanket
The sun	shone	as brightly as a beacon
The sun	singed the grass	like a torch

Choose the sentence or sentences that create the image you wish to paint for your reader. If you're thinking you can only use one of your new sentences, think again! With a little tweaking, several of the new similes can be blended into a paragraph that paints a vivid mental picture:

> At first, the sun heated the earth below like a warm, soft blanket. But as the fiery blaze climbed higher in the sky, its rays pressed us like a hot iron. The ground below, parched, dry, and lifeless, looked as if a torch had singed it.

Similes, like other types of figurative language, bring wonderful description to your writing. Creating similes with vivid action verbs is one way to eliminate "to be" verbs and add action as well as detail, imagery, and expression.

As a writer, you must be the judge of how many similes to use in a piece of writing. How much figurative language is too much? Similes season your writing in the same way that spices season your food. A little chili powder will give your chili its distinct flavor, but too much will ruin it! Like all types of figurative language, similes should be placed in your writing with the utmost care. If you read your work aloud, your ear will help you decide if you have "overdone" the similes.

See Figures 11.1 and 11.2 for examples of similes in action written by sixth-grade students.

Student Examples

                                                          Melanie

It was a hard boiled egg.
Eliminate <u>was</u>

<u>Subject</u>	<u>Vivid Action</u>	<u>Comparison</u>
The hard boiled egg	cracked in my hand	like a chip
The egg	slid from my hand	like butter
My hand	covered in slime from the egg,	looked like a slug
I	snatched a real egg	quicker than a sports car.
The egg	bursted	like a bubble.

   The hard boiled egg cracked in my hand like a chip.
The egg slid from my hand like butter.
My hand, covered in slime from the egg, looked like a slug.
   I snatched a real egg quicker than a sports car.
     The egg bursted in my hand like a bubble.

I will use:
   My hand, covered in slime from the egg, looked like a slug.

Fig. 11.1

CHAPTER ELEVEN: FIGURATIVE LANGUAGE MEETS RATIOCINATION

Jaden

Original Sentence: I was angry.
Eliminate: was

Subject	Vivid Action	Comparison
I	turned on my sister	like a rabid dog turning to attack
My head	almost exploded	like a volcano about to erupt
My heart	burst	like a lightbulb
My nails	dug into my arm	like a prarie dog burrowing in the dirt
My hands.	clenched into fists	like an armadillo curling into a ball.

My New Sentences:
I turned on my sister like a rabid dog turning to attack.
My head almost exploded like a volcano about to erupt.
My heart burst like a lightbulb cracking into a million pieces.
My nails dug into my arm like a prarie dog burrowing in the dirt.
My hands clenched into fists like an armadillo curling into a ball.

Sentence I will use in my paper:
My hands clenched into fists like an armadillo curling into a ball.

Fig. 11.2

PERSONIFICATION RATIOCINATION: REMOVE "TO BE" VERBS BY BREATHING LIFE INTO YOUR SUBJECTS

This strategy helps when students use forms of "to be" in sentences whose subjects are inanimate objects. Using personification helps weed out the "to be" verbs and adds action – and *life* – to sentences and stories.

EXAMPLE #1:

The willow tree by the river *was* tall. Target: Omit *was*

Begin by listing human actions the tree could perform.

Subject	Personification Verb
tree	leaned
tree	reached
tree	waited
tree	danced
tree	protected
tree	waved
tree	held

Continue brainstorming as many human action verbs as possible to *personify* the tree (subject).

Now create simple sentences to convey the original thought, removing the "to be" verbs and replacing them with verbs that show human actions. Be imaginative, and feel free to exaggerate!

The tall willow **leaned** down to the river.
The tall willow **reached** across the river.
The tall willow **waited** near the river.
The tall willow **danced** along the river's edge.

CHAPTER ELEVEN: FIGURATIVE LANGUAGE MEETS RATIOCINATION

Once students have chosen the action verbs that *personify* the subject in the most interesting and vivid ways, they add sensory details, adjectives, adverbs, and descriptive phrases to make the sentence "show" rather than merely "tell." Personification adds *action* to sentences; now, paint a picture by adding description.

The tall willow tree **leaned** gracefully across the narrow, winding river.
The willow tree, tall and graceful, **reached** longingly across the raging river.
The tall and graceful willow tree **waited** patiently along the side of the river.
The willow tree, gracefully bending downward, **danced** along the river's edge.

Choose which of the new sentences that best conveys the image you want readers to see.

EXAMPLE #2:

The wind **was** blowing. Target: Omit *was*.

List human actions the wind could perform.

Subject	Personification Verb
wind	moaned
wind	grabbed
wind	growled
wind	tickled
wind	pulled
wind	whispered

Create simple sentences with the new verbs:

The wind **moaned** all night.
The wind **grabbed** my hair.
The wind **growled** loudly.

> The wind *tickled* my face.

Now add adjectives, adverbs, phrases, and sensory details. Show, don't tell.

> The gusty wind *moaned* sorrowfully as the clock struck midnight.
> The soft wind *grabbed* my hair and swirled it in circles around me.
> A violent wind from the north *growled* in a low, earthy voice.
> A sudden warm wind *tickled* my face as I stood on the weathered, wooden porch.

Try reworking the structure of these new sentences into your writing. As with any type of figurative language, be selective.

Example:

> As I stood on the weathered, wooden porch, a sudden warm breeze tickled my face. It grew into a gusty wind that moaned sorrowfully. Growling in a low, earthy voice, it grabbed my hair, swirling it in circles around me. Through the half-open window, I heard the grandfather clock strike midnight.

See figures 11.3, 11.4, 11.5 for examples from Victor, Yasmin, and Madelyn.

CHAPTER ELEVEN: FIGURATIVE LANGUAGE MEETS RATIOCINATION

Student Name: Victor

Personification Ratiocination Thinking Sheet

Original Sentence: The moon was looking at us.

Target: Eliminate was

Subject	Personification Verb
The moon	glared
The moon	peeked
The moon	stared

Simple Sentences:

The moon glared at us.
The moon peeked at us.
The moon stared at us.

Elaborated Sentences: (Add adjectives, adverbs, phrases, and sensory details.)

The moon glared at the earth down below with a soft expression on its face.
The moon peeked from behind the clouds of the night catching a glimpse of the earth.
The moon stared down at us as it lit up the night sky.

Fig. 11.3

Student Samples

Yasmin

Personification

Original Sentence:
The wind is moving.
Target: is

Subject	Personification Verb
The wind	ran
The wind	danced
The wind	flowed
The wind	reached
The wind	moaned

Simple sentence:
The wind ran through red and yellow leaves.
The wind danced from tree to tree.
The wind flowed above the glittery water.
The wind reached down to the pile of leaves.
The wind sang me to sleep.

Elaborated Sentence:
The wind ran swiftly through a pile of colorful fall leaves.
The wind danced from tree to tree.
The wind flowed above the glittery water.
The wind reached down to kiss my silky hair.
The wind sang me a lullaby as I drowned to sleep.

Fig. 11.4

Chapter Eleven: Figurative Language Meets Ratiocination

Personification Rationation
Madelyn

Original Sentence:
The dandelion was by the lake.
Target: Eliminate *was*

Subject	Personification Verb
dandelion	danced
dandelion	leaned
dandelion	waited
dandelion	smiled
dandelion	waved

Simple Sentences:
The dandelion danced near the lake.
The dandelion leaned over the lake.
The dandelion waited by the lake.
The dandelion smiled at the lake next door.
The dandelion waved at the lake nearby.

Elaborated Sentences:
The dandelion danced gracefully near the lake.
A group of dandelions leaned over the clear, blue lake.
The white dandelion waited paitientally by the lake.
The dandelion smiled sweetly at the lake next door.
The dandelion waved at the lake nearby.

Fig. 11.5

And there you have it: Personification Ratiocination! Replace forms of "to be" with vivid, colorful action verbs that bring your subjects to life.

JEAN EWER HAWSEY earned her B.A. in Music Education Cum Laude from St. Mary's University in San Antonio, Texas, and her M.S. in Education from Walden University. She began her teaching career in middle-school choir and English. Hawsey has spent 20 years in the English classroom and believes teaching is the most important job anyone could have. Currently she teaches sixth grade in San Antonio. She has also taught preschool music, kindergarten, and elementary music, as well as private music lessons. She has played music professionally since high school. Hawsey loves poetry and songwriting, singing and playing guitar and piano, and of course, spending time with her wonderful family, close friends, and outstanding fellow educators in Northside ISD.

Chapter Twelve
Ratiocination: Supporting the Writing Life

Judy Wallis

As teachers of writing, our own rich, literate lives inform our teaching. A host of experts write about the insights gained when we engage in the writing life (Emig,1983; Elbow, 1983, Murray, 1996, and Carroll and Wilson, 2008). My own experiences as both teacher and writer have taught me the reciprocal nature of teaching and learning. I have discovered that as writers, we use unique, personal processes and share common patterns and needs.

Recently, I invited teachers in a summer workshop to join me as a writer. I find one of the most satisfying experiences for teachers is to be given time to write. To prepare, we explored the genre of memoir as readers, reading outstanding examples. We charted the attributes: their descriptions of time and place, the specificity of thoughts and feelings, and their attention to detail.

As we approached our writing, I thought aloud, considering my own possible topics. I selected a memorable time and began to draft a story from my childhood. I invited the teachers to confer with one another about their own possible topics and write their own stories. After a short public conference with one writer to model Elbow's "Say Back," the teachers shared their own writing in small groups. After some time to add fellow writers' responses to their writing, I collected their drafts. That evening, I word processed all the teachers' writing.

When the following morning arrived, the teachers received copies of their stories. My goal was to offer them an opportunity to refine a piece of writing they could share with students as they established a community of writers in their own classrooms in the fall. It was here ratiocination became a robust tool they could

Teacher Samples

use to refine their writing. They discovered firsthand the benefits and insights gained through the process. As we worked through clues, coding and decoding, teachers, just as our students, felt a sense of agency as they reentered their writing to revise.

We considered the following clues: sentence beginnings, "to be" verbs, and sentence variety. As I introduced each clue for coding, I used my own writing to model and considered the possible ways we might decode. The teachers worked individually and together as they coded and selected from the possibilities for decoding. Not only did teachers find their identify as writers, they also developed an appreciation for the revision process we all seem to dread as writers. The systematic nature of ratiocination offers strategic access to our own writing and yet preserves the whole-to-part-to-whole process we value. Some samples of the teachers' "before" and "after" writing follow.

An Excerpt of Kathy's "before" writing .

I fell in love with camping in 1967. Our family decided to camp in Colorado with my uncle's family. The two families rented a small pop-up camper and the ten of us drove to Colorado for a two-week vacation. I was excited as we entered the state of Colorado. There was a blue outline of the Rocky Mountains on the western horizon! We visited many old west towns and attractions. I was happy to be in Colorado. Every night our little pop-up camper was set up. The adults and young children (at 8 years old I was one of them) slept in the pop-up, while my older sister, brother, and cousin slept in a tent.

Chapter Twelve: Supporting the Writing Life

An Excerpt of Kathy's "after" writing...

When I was young, I fell in love with camping. In 1967, our family decided to camp in Colorado with my uncle's family. The two families rented a small pop-up camper, and the ten of us drove to Colorado for a two-week vacation. I will always remember my excitement as we entered the state of Colorado, and I saw the blue outline of the Rocky Mountains on the western horizon! We visited many old west towns and attractions while in Colorado and every night we set up our little pop-up camper. The adults and young children (at 8 years old I was one of them) slept in the pop-up, while my older sister, brother, and cousin slept in a tent.

Kris' "before" writing . . .

When I was three, I had an overwhelming desire to go to school. I would wake up early and run outside to play with my friends. They waited for their bus, but I was left alone waving to them as the bus drove away.

One morning, Alana, my best friend's sister, had a fantastic idea. She decided I could pretend to be her cousin from California. I'd go to school with her that day. I thought this was the best idea ever! I got on the bus that morning and we went to school.

Once we arrived at school, I met the teacher, Mrs. Rosemeier. I exclaimed, "Hi, my name is Kristi and I am Alana's cousin from California!" Mrs. Rosemeier welcomed me and then asked me my phone number. I

told her, "546-7483" and went off to play with the other children.

A short time later, my mom and baby brother showed up at the school. I hadn't told my mom where I was going. I was quite perplexed how she found out. I could tell she wasn't very happy and knew I was probably in for a bit of trouble. She grabbed my hand, thanked the teacher, and back home we went.

It wasn't until years later that I discovered it was giving her my very local phone number that had given me away. My first day of school didn't last very long, but it was one to remember!

Kris's "after" writing . . .

When I was three, I had an overwhelming desire to go to school. Every morning, I would wake up early and run outside to play with my friends as they waited for their bus. And, every morning I was left alone waving to them as the bus drove away.

One morning, Alana, my best friend's sister, had a fantastic idea. I would pretend to be her cousin from California and go to school with her that day. I thought this was the best idea ever! Without any further thought, I got on the bus that morning and off to school we went.

Once we arrived at school, Alana took me right to her classroom and brought me up to her kindergarten teacher, Mrs. Rosemeier. I went straight up to her and exclaimed, "Hi, my name is Kristi and I am Alana's cousin from California!" Mrs. Rosemeier welcomed me warmly and then, with great wisdom, asked me my phone number. With great pride, I told her, "546-7483" and went off to play with the other children.

A short time later, my mom and baby brother showed up at the school. I hadn't told my mom where I was going, so I was quite perplexed

CHAPTER TWELVE: SUPPORTING THE WRITING LIFE

as to how she found out. From the look on her face, I could tell she wasn't very happy and I was probably in for a bit of trouble. She grabbed my hand, thanked the teacher, and back home we went.

It wasn't until years later that I discovered it was my proud delivery of my very local phone number that had given me away. My first day of school didn't last very long, but it was one to remember!

These teachers shared examples of the revisions they made and conferred with table partners. Because I'd saved the stories as a file, teachers could go immediately to the computer and make revisions. In less than two days, we'd gone from studying memoir as a form to writing our own stories and publishing them. *When We Were Young* became not only a product to be shared with others, it also offered the promise of this "elegant solution" to that final phase of writing so many of us dread. The teachers left committed to being both writers and teachers of writing. This experience speaks to the power of insights we gain from authentic experiences as both teacher and learner. The view becomes so much clearer.

REFERENCES

Carroll, Joyce Armstrong & Edward E. Wilson. *Acts of Teaching: How to Teach Writing* (2nd ed). Westport, Connecticut: Teacher Idea Press, 2008.

Emig, Janet. *The Web of Meaning.* Upper Montclair, NJ: Boynton/Cook Publishers, 1983.

Elbow, Peter and Pat Belanoff. *Sharing and Responding*. New York: Random House, 1989.

Murray, Donald. *Crafting a Life in Essay, Story, Poem.* Portsmouth, NH: Boynton/Cook Publishers, 1966.

JUDY WALLIS has spent the past four decades as a teacher, literacy coach, staff developer, and university instructor. She served two large, diverse, Houston, Texas school districts as language arts director and provided leadership support for literacy coaches for twenty-one years. Her professional interests and work focus on leadership and whole-school/district change through robust literacy instruction. She currently teaches at the University of Houston and works with schools and districts around the country as a staff developer and educational consultant.

Coda
The Legacy of Ratiocination

Because ratiocination is my "baby," I am intensely interested in its progress. I have taught it and observed it from pre-K through high school. Then I took it to college where I taught it for almost twenty years. The Abydos trainers who are college professors have also introduced ratiocination in college. But, I wondered, how does my "baby" fare in college and beyond when their professors do not invite ratiocination? Kim Carlton, Instructional Specialist, Richardson High School and bronze level Abydos trainer posted a call on her Facebook to help me find out. Following are some responses she received and sent on to me. While some may not recall the name "ratiocination," it is clear they remember and—most importantly—use the concept. Ratiocination lives, it has roots, a history, and a legacy.

dr jac

- Whenever I wrote a long paper, either research or fiction, I used the highlighting techniques we did for our book report--then print a copy and look for one particular thing at a time way. Looked for "be" verbs, sentence length, etc. and edited the paper accordingly [ratiocination]. I just started doing that with the story I'm writing on my free time, and I'm actually using that technique [ratiocination] as I polish up my grad school application papers :). Hope this helps!

–Amanda (Evergreen College and now working for the Washington State House of Representatives)

- You taught me that contrary to what I had learned in 7-9th grade, there is in fact NO law that says an essay must have 5 (and only 5!!) paragraphs. You taught me to write directly and confidently, as if I knew everything I was saying was true (even if I wasn't 100% sure that I was making sense). You also taught me how to strengthen my writing be checking for and eliminating passive voice [ratiocination] (a concept no other teacher has mentioned to this day). I guess one last thing you taught me is that research papers are a lot more palatable if you can write about something that you find interesting, not just some b.s. that you think is easy. Hope that helps!

—Kelly O-W

- Ratiocination was a great tool for the improvement of my writing techniques. Not only did it help the editing process, but it has gradually been incorporated into my initial drafts. I notice errors and redundancies throughout the writing process. Basically, ratiocination has become an unnoticed part of the way I write, which should be its ultimate goal.

—Trey

- I have learned so much being in the Creative Writing class. My only regret is that the class is not a full year course, because I would love to have it next semester as well. I learned techniques for writing [ratiocination] that are not only helpful to me now but will also be helpful to me at Wake Forest University. When we begin to work on a piece, my teacher creates one as well. When we edit, she edits. When we submit for publication, she also sends a piece in. Her full participation not only shows her dedication to teaching but also her true enjoyment of writing.

—Kelly G

At fifteen, I thought I was a literary master. Spelling, grammar, reading and writing have always come naturally to me. I never wrote a paper that received less than an A. Truthfully, I was quasi-English snob.

I would often write a paper and print it out without so much as a glance over for errors. I felt that editing was a tedious chore reserved for student who didn't possess the same English skills as me. It wasn't until I entered Ms. Carlton's sophomore English class that I realized that a good writer revises their work, and then revises again.

A typical paper for Ms. Carlton's class always began with a round of minilessons centered on improving our essays. She introduced us to a new term, ratiocination. Ratiocination involves different techniques, layered upon each other, to improve a paper. One lesson would have us circle all of the "to-be" verbs, and another would have us searching for pronouns. By using the different ratiocination techniques, Ms. Carlton informed us that we would vastly improve our writing skills.

I approached my revision with an air of flippancy. Surely my document editor caught all of my spelling and grammar mistakes. I knew the conventions of English—what more did I need to edit?

Ms. Carlton's lesson over commas had us highlighting all of the commas in our papers. Afterwards, we were supposed to go back and decide the necessity of each one and reduce them by half. I never really knew that you could overuse commas. I was mistaken. My paper was bleeding yellow highlighter after I was finished editing. I was astonished—wasn't every single comma absolutely justified when it came to the integrity of the paper? The answer was, no. They weren't. I was too liberal with my commas. By over using commas, I was slowing down the pace of my paper, therefore making it more tedious to read.

I had an epiphany that morning in Ms. Carlton's English class. I realized that in order for me to be a good writer, I needed to be aware that editing is important. Now, even as a college student, I make sure to take my time while writing my papers. In fact, to this day, I still go through my papers and highlight each comma to ensure the necessity

Coda: The Legacy of Ratiocination

of each one.

    Ms. Carlton has had a big influence in my life—because of her, I have realized my ultimate life's goal to become a teacher. I attribute my skills as an English major to the ratiocination techniques that I learned as a sophomore in high school. Her enthusiasm and writing system has stuck with me through the years. Even as I write, I'm glancing through and mentally highlighting all of my commas.

—Wendy